History TODAY

Rowland Hill
'The second Whitefield'

Tim Shenton

DayOne

ISBN 978-1-84625-636-3

British Library Cataloguing in Publication Data available

Published by Day One Publications
Ryelands Road, Leominster, HR6 8NZ
Telephone 01568 613 740
Toll Free 888 329 6630 (North America)
email—sales@dayone.co.uk
web site—www.dayone.co.uk

Printed by 4edge Limited

Commendations on Tim Shenton's larger work on Rowland Hill (*The life of Rowland Hill: the second Whitefield*), on which this book is based, include:

'Here is biography at its best. Shenton marvellously brings Rowland Hill to life in a balanced and objective way, neither minimizing his remarkable set of gifts nor hiding his destructive blemishes. How humble and spiritual he was! How arresting was his preaching style, with all its pathos, vivid illustrations and ready wit! How many wonderful divine interventions attended his ministry! The stories of God's grace and striking applications of individual statements made by Hill abound in these pages without ever resorting to hagiography. Perhaps it is this combination that makes this biography such a fascinating read. You will find no dull pages in the book.'

Joel R. Beeke
Puritan Reformed Theological Seminary
Grand Rapids, Michigan

'This book by Tim Shenton is a delight. We are given an excellent portrayal of Rowland Hill, the man, his times and his achievements under God, as well as fresh incentive for praise to God and prayer that he might raise up like men in our day of small things.'

Dr Michael A. G. Haykin
Principal and Professor of Church History and Reformed Spirituality, Toronto Baptist
Seminary, Toronto

'In this exceptional biography we are introduced to a colourful character in a lively way. The courage and commitment, as well as the eccentricities and indiscretions, of this remarkable preacher are set out with an honesty for which the author is to be commended. Here, so much to be learned, is contained in a most enjoyable read—a must for the library of every serious Christian.'

Brian H. Edwards
Christian author, lecturer and teacher

Commendations

'Through careful research and with an objectivity that is often missing in evangelical biographies, Tim Shenton has produced a definitive biography of this complex evangelical leader. This massive and extensive work will introduce Hill to a new generation of readers. Written in a lively and engaging style, *The life of Rowland Hill* makes a vital contribution to the study of English society in the eighteenth century.'

ICM books direct

'Once again Tim Shenton blows us away with a great read about a powerhouse of evangelical Christianity, the British preacher Rowland Hill. Thoroughly researched and written with a deeply interesting style. The story of Hill's life and ministry are thoroughly interesting so that we are left wanting more. Thanks to Tim Shenton for another inspiring read. Christians everywhere are indebted to him.'

Dr Jay Hines
The American Gospel Hour Radio Program

Contents

I am appreciative of Day One for their enthusiasm to produce this abridgement of my book *Rowland Hill, the second Whitefield*, published by Reformation Heritage Books. I realise that my original work of over 700 pages is not everyone's 'cup of tea', the sheer length being enough to put off many readers. Rowland Hill is such an important, yet neglected character in the history of the church that it would be an injustice to the great man if his work and character were bypassed simply because a book is too long.

So my principal motivation in producing this shorter work is to bring Rowland Hill to the notice of a wider readership, who might otherwise have rejected a 'heavy tome'. However, I admit that a second reason for writing this abridgement is that it might whet the appetite of some readers, who will then want to delve into the complete version, which at the time of writing is still in print.

Be assured that the present volume follows the same scholarship and research as the original, although all references, the bibliography and index have been omitted. I have tried to concentrate on Rowland Hill the preacher, and have only briefly touched on the other areas of his eventful and influential life. As most people 'love a story' I have retained many of the anecdotes that fill the original volume.

The task of reducing an important historical work of 700 pages down to its present size is not easy and there have been many occasions when I have wrestled with what not to include. For someone whose natural instinct is to include the smallest detail this has at times been a bit like cutting off a limb. Having said that, I have tried to retain everything that is *essential* to Rowland Hill's story.

Tim Shenton
April 2019

1. Born again

There are three men, who are the most powerful preachers that England has ever produced, and yet only two of them are well known. The first is George Whitefield, commonly regarded as 'one of the greatest figures in modern evangelism' and rightly brought to the forefront by Arnold Dallimore's excellent two-volume biography, first published in 1970. The third is Charles Spurgeon, the prince of preachers, of whom many would agree with Carl F. H. Henry's summary, when he called him 'one of evangelical Christianity's immortals'.

Rowland Hill

But who is the preacher between these two heroes? Who links them both together? Who was it that Lady Huntingdon wrote about with such godly enthusiasm, when she said, 'The crowds that follow him wherever he is called to preach, overwhelm me with astonishment... Dear Captain Joss told me above a hundred awakened souls, the fruits of his preaching, have been received into the Tabernacle Society... I have attended him at Blackheath and Kennington, where the Lord blessed his testimony in a very remarkable manner. Thousands and thousands attended, and the most awful and solemn impressions seemed to pervade the vast assemblies. Excepting my beloved and lamented Mr Whitefield, I never witnessed any person's preaching wherein there were such displays of the Divine power and glory. May HE who hath raised up this *second Whitefield*, with talents and zeal so distinguished, make him eminent in his day and generation, crown his message with success.'

This 'second Whitefield' of whom the Countess spoke, and who took up Whitefield's mantle when that great man died in 1770, just as Elisha took up Elijah's mantle, was Rowland Hill.

****

Rowland Hill was born at Hawkstone in Shropshire on 23 August 1744. He was one of six sons born to Sir Rowland Hill of Hawkstone, who was sheriff of Shropshire in 1732 and elected a member of parliament for the city of Lichfield in 1734 and 1740. Rowland's mother, Lady Hill, was the daughter of Sir Brian Broughton. Rowland's eldest brother Richard was born in 1733. He became well known as the author of *Pietas Oxoniensis*, published in support of the six men who were expelled from Oxford University in 1768.

When Rowland was a boy he was lively in manner and high-spirited. Once he was brought into the room where his father and mother and some friends were enjoying a conversation, when someone said to him playfully, 'Well, Rowley, and what should you like to be?' He turned towards his father who was sitting in an armchair and said somewhat cheekily, 'I should like to be a baronet, and sit in a great chair.' He was observant of the things around him and his family enjoyed his original and jolly remarks. In later life he often referred with pleasure to the amusing incidents of his childhood and in his own inimitable style would relate the stories his mother had told him of the mischievous pranks he got up to before school. His character even as a child was frank and open, without reserve and entirely honest.

Rowland's early education was at the Royal Free Grammar School in Shrewsbury, which was founded by Edward VI. He then attended Eton, where he was surrounded by many temptations. In the last sermon he preached, when he urged sinners to run to the Redeemer, he looked back to his early days at Eton: 'You are not farther from God than Saul of Tarsus was; you are not farther off from God than I was when first I went to Eton school; there was never a sinner fonder of this world, or farther from the fear of God, than I was then; but God made me wise by his own power.'

His early religious impressions came from reading Isaac Watts's hymns for children, which were given to him by a Christian lady. These impressions were strengthened when his brother Richard read to him a sermon by Bishop Beveridge. It is said that his brother used to place his hand on his shoulder and exclaim, 'Rowland, Rowland, if you do not repent, and believe on the Lord Jesus Christ, you will be eternally lost.'

At this time Rowland also experienced deep distress when he recollected the words, 'The end of these things is death.' He may have been referring to the same period when, much later in life, preaching at Surrey Chapel from 2 Corinthians 1:12, he cried, 'Oh! Dear, I remember when I was sent to school what a wicked creature I was; but the grace of God, in his infinite mercy, met with me, and I began to see my own wickedness, and the wickedness of other youths of the same form.' These early convictions and conceptions of the truths of Christianity were so genuine and distinct that he never forgot them, and they were the beginning of the change that was to make such an impact on his life.

Richard spoke to Rowland again in the Christmas holidays of 1761, with the sincere intention of winning him to Christ. Then after he had returned to Eton he wrote to him and his brother Robert the following earnest letter, 'with a single view of promoting the salvation of our precious immortal souls'. It is dated 'London, 11 February 1762', when Rowland was only seventeen:

Surely, whilst we have the Bible in our hands, we can never be deluded to think that God can be pleased with the externals of religion whilst our hearts are far from him. No! The Scripture assures us, that none but those who have seen their lost state by nature, and who are made the children of God by faith in Jesus Christ, shall ever inherit the promises; and oh! how dreadful is the thought, to be cast out for ever and ever from the presence of God, into that lake which burneth with fire and brimstone, where their worm dieth not, and their fire is not quenched: where there is weeping and gnashing of teeth.

The seed sown by his brother and watered by his eldest sister Jane took root and began to grow. In the same month as the above letter Richard sent him the Works of Archbishop Leighton, from which Rowland derived great benefit. These books were preceded by another letter, in which Richard hoped Rowland would be enabled, by the grace of God 'to relish, digest and practise the divine truths' in Leighton's Works. He exhorted his brother to be

…frequent and earnest in prayer for fresh supplies of knowledge, faith, grace and strength…

Learn then to guard against self dependence, and to live more upon Christ… Resign yourself to him in all his offices, as a Prophet, Priest and King: a Prophet, to teach you; a Priest, to make atonement for you; a King, to reign over you, and in you…

Consider, my dear brother, how that when you, as a poor helpless sheep, were gone astray, this dear Shepherd sought you, and brought you back… O think of this 'love which passeth knowledge', and may it fill your heart with praise, and your tongue with thanksgiving. Let it constrain you to live to Him who died for you, and to grow daily more and more in conformity to his blessed image.

Rowland thought very highly of this letter and carefully preserved it, and in April 1794 sent a copy of it to the *Evangelical Magazine*, in the hope that what had been a blessing to him, might be profitable to some young persons in a similar situation. 'It was written,' he remarked in a note sent with the letter, 'to me by my brother, Sir Richard, when I was first called to the knowledge of the truth, being at that time a boy at Eton school.'

Soon after he reached the age of eighteen, Rowland entered his Master's 'sweet service', as he often termed his conversion. Interestingly, when he was preaching at the anniversary of a dissenting meeting, a few miles out of London, only a short time before his death, he spoke passionately to the young people present about remembering their Creator in the days of their youth; then, after mentioning the advantages that would result from it, he said, 'I gave myself up to God when I was only sixteen years of age, and I have never yet repented of doing so, nor do I think I ever shall.' Rowland was mistaken about his age.

He was fond of illustrating his conversion by the story of a poor Negro, who had been kindly treated by his employer. After he had been working for him for some time, the master said to him,

'Now you are of age, you may go where you please, and serve any master you think proper. I did not buy you to keep you as a slave, but that you might enjoy the sweets of liberty. You can leave my house tomorrow, if you like.'

The poor slave was melted by the power of kindness, and, with the deepest emotion, he exclaimed, 'Me leave you, my dear massa; oh! not for de world. Me want no wages to serve you; if massa turn me out at one door, me will come in at de oder.'

In reference to his conversion, he said, 'I have never regretted that I went too young to the dear Redeemer; but I have often regretted that I did not go to him much earlier than I did.'

Rowland's growth in divine knowledge and experience brought much joy to Richard. The apathy and evil example of his fellow pupils only seemed to strengthen Rowland's resolve to follow Christ. He ignored their sneers and ridicule, and declared to them, with the passion of an ardent 'first love', what God had done in his soul, and by the grace of God was instrumental, even at this early stage in his religious career, in the conversion of some of them, the first fruits of an abundant harvest he was to reap later in life. Edwin Sidney remarked that the remembrance of these young converts 'shed a beam of peace and joy over the entire course of his long protracted journey through life'.

In a letter simply signed 'A Christian', the author points to Rowland's time at Eton and the zeal he displayed, remarking, 'He used to get up before his school-fellows, and run to the morning prayers of the church, from which he could return in time for the meeting of the school. His pocket money was always used for the relief of the poor, and his leisure hours were spent in visiting the distressed, and alleviating their sorrows, in which his sympathizing breast took a near part.'

On one occasion at Eton, he was so fervent in his witness to a female servant who frequently waited on him, that she rebuked him for his zeal and said that persons should not be 'righteous over much' and should be 'careful to avoid extremes in religion'. She went on to say that 'some were too cold, and some were too hot'. Young Rowland responded immediately, with the adroitness for which he became well known, 'Then I suppose you think that we had better be lukewarm?' 'Yes,' she said, 'that was the proper medium.' He then picked up the Bible and read Jesus' words to the church at Laodicea: 'I would thou wert cold or hot. So then, because thou art lukewarm, and neither cold nor hot, I will spew thee out of my mouth;' at which 'his tepid admonisher seemed a little surprised and aghast'.

Later in life he liked to visit Eton and he referred to a prayer meeting held in a cottage, which, after leaping a ditch with the help of a pole, he used to attend. The old woman who lived in the cottage was the recipient of his generosity till the day of her death. The Eton boys went to the Independent Chapel at Windsor to hear him preach in his old age, which greatly pleased him, and once the people were amused when they heard the boys alter the words: 'When rolling years shall cease to move', to 'When Rowland Hill shall cease to move'. After supper, he would say to his friends, 'The old man must go to bye bye.' He would then kneel down and address his Father with the reverence and love of a little child, 'Thou knowest that we are very sleepy,' before offering a short prayer.

The next morning he would go down to the barracks, to breakfast with one of his military nephews, and then come back full of fun, to relate exchanges of wit which had passed between the two... On taking leave of his host at Windsor, as the carriage and horses stood at the door, he said, pointing to the Royal Chapel and then at the steeds, whom he called 'Doctor Order and Doctor Decorum', 'Do you think you could get stalls for them up there? They have for many years been serving the Great Master, by dragging me through the country preaching the glorious gospel.'

While at Eton, Rowland frequently displayed the wit and humour for which he was to become well known and which made him such an interesting and lively conversationalist. There was once a debate among the students about the letter H. Some argued that it had the full power of a letter, while others thought it was a 'mere aspirate', and could be omitted altogether, without any disadvantage to the English language. Rowland earnestly contended for it to be kept, adding light-heartedly, 'To me the letter H is a most invaluable one, for if it be taken away, I shall be ill all the days of my life.'

In May 1764, while he was still at Eton, he visited some friends in London and attended the birthday celebrations of his cousin, in which there was 'dancing and all manner of carnality'. He refused to attend at first, but was persuaded to go in order not to give offence. Many of the guests danced for two hours before tea, enough to give Rowland 'a surfeit of it', although he did not join in.

While in the metropolis Rowland attended every sermon that was preached at the Lock and every Thursday he went to St Dunstan's to hear William Romaine. 'I have many obligations to the great Mr Romaine,' he wrote, 'who has often invited me and my companions to his house, where we often meet by eight in the morning. O how sweetly does he pray with us, teach and exhort us. Every word that comes from his mouth ought to be writ in letters of gold upon our hearts.' Romaine told him that in London 'many daily are added to the Church such as shall be saved'.

As his Eton days drew to a close, Rowland was anxious to become a preacher of the gospel, and his desire was to enter university with that end in mind. He was therefore delighted when he heard from his sister that Sir Rowland Hill was determined to send him to Cambridge. It was an important stepping-stone to his appointed goal.

2. 'Such a marked and hated person'

Rowland Hill as a young man

Sir Rowland's intention in sending his son to Cambridge was that he should obtain a fellowship at St John's and so become qualified for presentation to one of the family livings in Norfolk. At that time there were six livings in Norfolk in the gift of the Hill family, all of considerable value, with the restriction that they could only be presented to fellows of St John's College, Cambridge. Rowland was happy to go along with his father's design and so entered college as a pensioner. Subsequent events, however, changed Rowland's views and he became a fellow commoner and therefore was not eligible to fellowships.

Soon after he entered university, he wrote to his sister and mentioned the trials he was enduring and the religious opinions he held, opinions which changed little during his long ministry. He was grateful to the Lord that before he went to Cambridge, 'a barren and dry land where no water is', the Lord taught him 'all necessary truth'. Yet he complained that his trials 'both inward and outward' were great and he felt very much alone.

But now I am all in darkness, my prayers are faithless, consequently fruitless, my corruptions overwhelm me and almost drive me to despair. In this distress I have none for my counsellor, neither have I faith to go to Christ. Thus do I spend hours in tears; thus, in my distress and solitude, which I am ashamed to relate, I am driven even amongst worldly company for relief; and though perpetual solitude, I find, hurts my soul very much, yet worldly company is still more prejudicial.

He had difficulties 'greater than human nature is able to encounter with, to surmount', and called out loudly for his sister's pity, prayers and advice. At the same time he realised that he needed to be 'tried in the furnace of affliction', and to be cleansed from his 'very much dross'. It was probably the correspondence with his brother and sister that kept him from being overwhelmed by his inward and outward conflicts at this time.

At home his religious views displeased his parents, especially his seeming indifference to the establishment, but at least Richard and Jane were prepared to defend him. Lady Huntingdon also wrote to his parents on two occasions interceding on his behalf. He was defended too by a pious nobleman, who was a frequent visitor to Hawkstone and much respected by Sir Rowland and Lady Hill. However, it was at university that he fought the real battle, and would often say, when looking back to those 'dark days' that on account of his religion he was 'such a marked and hated person, that nobody belonging to the college ever gave him a cordial smile, except the old shoe black at the gate, who had the love of Christ in his heart'.

News of his zeal for the gospel soon reached the ears of John Berridge of Everton, who wrote to him from Grantchester, which is only a mile from Cambridge (Rowland once swam against the current from Cambridge to Grantchester). He asked Rowland to walk over to see him, saying, 'The weather is frosty, which makes it pleasant under foot.' He concluded his note with words that lifted Rowland's spirits: 'If you love Jesus Christ, you will not be surprised at this freedom taken with you by a stranger, who seeks your acquaintance only out of his love to Christ and his people.' Rowland

John Berridge

immediately accepted with joy the invitation, and thus started a close friendship between the two men.

Every Sunday regardless of the weather Rowland rode from Cambridge to Berridge's church, hurrying back in time for the college chapel. On one occasion he wrote, 'Many a mile have I ridden, many a storm have I faced, many a snow have I gone through, to hear good old Mr Berridge; for I felt his ministry, when in my troubles at Cambridge, a comfort and blessing to my soul. Dear affectionate old man. I love him to my heart.' The Christmas of 1764 he spent with his new friend at Everton and met many people whose religious views were similar to his own. There is no doubt that the private counsels of Berridge were useful to Rowland—'like an oasis in the spiritual desert of his college life'—though it is to be feared that Berridge's eccentricities strengthened 'those peculiar traits' in Rowland's own character, 'which occasionally led him to forget the sanctity of the pulpit'.

Despite these encouragements, Rowland was greatly troubled at this time, and he often lay awake at night, refusing to be comforted. On one of these sleepless nights he composed a poem about his salvation, which he wrote down the next morning. It is dated 29 May 1765, the first three verses of which are:

My guilty soul, how long beset
With terrors all around,
Whilst law and justice claimed their debt,
And I no payment found.

In works and duties long I tried,
Some inward peace to find,
The more I strove, the more I cried,
Ah! much is left behind.

At length I heard the gospel sound,
O joyful sound to me!
Jehovah just may still be found,
And set the ungodly free.

In accordance with the advice of Berridge and other friends, Rowland started to preach the gospel. His first effort appears to have been in a cottage on his father's estate, where he explained parts of the Bible to the poor people. He afterwards preached in several places in Cambridge and in nearby villages, and, accompanied by Thomas Pentycross, David Simpson and others, visited the sick, workhouses and jails, calling sinners to repentance. On one of these occasions he met a young man, who was about to be executed for robbery. 'After I had prayed, and another young man

Thomas Pentycross

(Mr Pentycross...); I asked him, before the executioner came out for his body to be hung up at the [prison] door, "Can you give me any hope that God has answered our prayers and broken your heart?" The poor man, rattling his chains, being fast bound in misery and iron, burst into tears, and said, "Oh, Sir, my heart is as hard as stone."' The criminal's answer made a deep impression on Rowland and he frequently mentioned it for the rest of his life when appealing to sinners.

David Simpson

As can be imagined such unusual 'visiting' from an undergraduate brought down on him the severest censure from his college, and insults from the populace of the town. At length the opposition became so serious that Rowland wrote to George Whitefield for advice. He received a reply on 27 December 1766, which is important in regard to his future ministry.

George Whitefield

About thirty four years ago, the master of Pembroke College, where I was educated, took me to task for visiting the sick and going to the prisons. In my haste I said, 'Sir, if it displeaseth you I will go no more:' my heart smote me immediately—I repented and went again—he heard of it—threatened—but for fear he should be looked upon as a persecutor, let me alone—the hearts of all are in the Redeemer's hands. I would not have you give way, no not for a moment—the storm is too great to hold long—visiting the sick and imprisoned, and instructing the ignorant, are the very vitals of true and undefiled religion. If threatened, denied degree, or expelled for this, it will be the best degree you can take. A glorious preparative for, and a blessed passage of future usefulness. I have seen the dreadful consequences of giving way and looking back. How many by this wretched cowardice and fear of the cross have been turned into pillars, not of useful, but of useless salt!... Now is the time to prove the strength of Jesus yours. If opposition did not so much abound, your consolations would not so abound. Blind as he is, Satan sees some great good coming on.

Whitefield assured Rowland that 'old Berridge' would give him the same advice.

The clarity and boldness of Whitefield's response was just what Rowland wanted to hear, and he decided to defy all resistance from whatever quarter. In April 1767, Whitefield set out from Brighton for Norwich, and visited Rowland and his society at Cambridge on his way.

Rowland encouraged the fellow students in his club to follow Christ wholeheartedly and to press on through all the obstacles that were thrown down before them. His parents strongly opposed his actions and his superiors in the university condemned all he did. It was hinted that his testimonials and even his degree would be refused if he continued his irregularities, but he was too determined to serve Christ to give in to threats, and nor could he see how his breach of university regulations would hinder his future usefulness.

Not only was his fiery and fearless temperament upholding him at this time, but the stirring letters of his friend George Whitefield, who wrote to him again on 4 June 1767, calling him 'my dear professor', and told him how 'thousands and thousands' attended his own preaching in Gloucestershire and South Wales. He then exhorted, 'Fear not to go without the camp—keep open the correspondence between the two universities. Remember the praying legions—they were never known to yield… God be your physician under your bodily malady! A thorn—a thorn—but Christ's grace will be sufficient for you.'

When Rowland arrived home his sister Jane and brother Richard, who had recently become a village preacher and a visitor of prisons like himself, warmly welcomed him; but his parents were far from pleased with his 'religion'. It was rumoured that they insisted on him giving up his 'erratic career', and threatened that he would be excluded from the family circle if he persisted in this nonsense. He respectfully but firmly argued for liberty of conscience and found consolation and strength in the words: 'When my father and my mother forsake me, then the Lord will take me up.' He often used to speak of his 'sorrowful walks amidst the beautiful scenery of his father's grounds, and of the frowns which pierced to the very core of his tender and affectionate heart'. He said, 'Hawkstone is now a furnace indeed.'

On account of his 'religion', his father only allowed him a small annual income, which meant that he often travelled in his Master's service without a shilling in his pocket and without knowing in the morning where he was going to rest that night. His mother, it seems, was his strongest foe. Towards the end of his life, he was walking on the terrace at Hawkstone, when he mentioned to a lady who was with him, 'In my youth I have often paced this spot bitterly weeping; while by most of the inhabitants of yonder house, I was considered as a disgrace to my family. But,' he added with tears streaming down his aged face, 'it was for the cause of my God.'

Rowland took every opportunity to speak of Christ to his family, although the occasions were few and far between. However, he rejoiced when his brother Brian was converted and received congratulations from Whitefield.

In spite of this much needed encouragement, Rowland was finding the opposition of his parents and the obstacles that were thrown in his way difficult to handle. There is no doubt that his spirits were dampened at this stage of his Cambridge career.

3. Friends and foes

Through George Whitefield's intervention it was determined that Rowland should visit Lady Huntingdon at Bath on his way from Hawkstone to Cambridge. With that purpose in mind, Rowland commended to God those he was about to leave and on 21 October 1767 he started his journey south. The following day, Whitefield, writing to John Fletcher, alluded to the troubles at Cambridge, when he said, 'There is hot work at Cambridge. One dear youth is likely to be expelled. Mr Lee is suspended without admonition, or having a moment's warning.' Luke Tyerman rightly noted that Rowland at Cambridge was 'evincing courage hardly inferior to that of the first Oxford Methodists. Without courting persecution, he was not afraid of it.'

Lady Huntingdon

Lady Huntingdon had been following events at Cambridge with interest and was anxious to meet Rowland and to talk with him about what the Lord was doing. Earlier in the year Lady Anne Erskine had written to Jane Hill, requesting that her brother Richard 'send an exact account as he can of the young men with Rowl[e]y who are in or going into orders, as Lady H. has a promise of recommending to Dr Lee a lecturer for the great church at Halifax, a thing of the greatest consequence'. When Rowland arrived at Bath, the Countess welcomed him 'with open arms', as she herself put it. He preached in her chapel and expounded in her house 'with much comfort'.

Lady Huntingdon showed Rowland maternal kindness in his season of distress and anxiety, and supported him in whatever way she could, which is evident from the following letter:

He was as my own son—received into my house, and preached in my pulpits. I have again written to Lady Hill in his behalf, my former application to Sir Rowland having met with no redress. But they obstinately refuse to answer any letter I write to entreat for him. There is no hope then from that quarter... I have a confidence, a firm persuasion that he will triumph; for he is on the Lord's side, and Jesus, the King of Zion will enable him to overcome every obstacle intended to retard the progress of his truth, in preventing his entrance into orders... He has preached frequently, and great crowds attended at the chapel and at my house. His word fell with great power, and some were pierced to the heart.

Rowland arrived back in Cambridge and soon started to preach. Some of his friends, who shared his religious sentiments and principles, considered his irregular course as unsuitable preparation for his degree and harmful to a future ministry. On the one hand, there were Whitefield's supporters, who rejoiced at Rowland's activities and at having a man of his connections, talents, character and influence on their side. On the other hand, a group of his friends called his Methodism immethodical. Augustus Toplady, who thought of him very highly, felt alarmed and displeased—alarmed because he feared his eccentric spirit might lead him to depart from the articles and homilies of the Church of England, as well as its disciplines and rules; and displeased because he had so openly sanctioned the principle of dissent from the national establishment. Predictably, Rowland refused to budge from his course.

His situation at the university and his feelings are described in a letter he wrote to Whitefield on 12 May 1768.

Blessed be God, we are not without being steeped more than ever in shame in this place... Though we always endeavour to keep clear of a mob, in letting no more know than our different houses will hold, yet in spite of all that can be done, more or less of the gown constantly attend... They have hitherto always stood like poor brow beaten things with much attention till we have done, when they generally get together to compare notes, which they afterwards retail among others of the university dressed up in a droll fashion, well embellished with the addition of many ludicrous lies. This makes all as I pass the streets stop to wonder at me as a strange oddity.

He mentioned four gownsmen who never missed a meeting and who always spoke respectfully of the word. Many others were convinced of the truth, while some, 'filled with the hottest madness, dress me up as a fool, and cudgel me as a knave'. One night, the mob of the gown caused such a disturbance at the house where Rowland and his friends were meeting, that the constable was forced to attend 'that no riot might ensue'. Rowland decided that it would be prudent to be 'more private the next time, and be contented with a house full, attended only with a few gownsmen by way of bringing up the rear'.

The doctors at the university, realising that Rowland only had a short while to stay, came to the following compromise: 'that I am to continue to be possessor of my *professorship*, and to be still bishop over all their parishes, provided I will be contented with houses or barns, and leave them alone with quiet possession of their streets, fields and churches, and by and bye they will be glad to sign my *testimonium*, in order to get rid of me'. He was hoping to make good a promise he had made to one who asked him 'when we enthusiasts intended to stop?'—his reply being, 'not at all till such time as we have carried all before us'.

Immediately after taking his degree he wrote to his sister. He mentioned the 'furnace' he had been in and the 'many enemies' he had made, but his consolation was that *'the Lord is King'*. His tutor wanted him to stay at the college, and to this request his master at first agreed, but then seemed to change his mind, insisting that if he was to stay he had to promise *'never to make any more converts in the University*, or never going into any house in the town even to relieve the piteous, but that I must give all my alms into the hands of others to dispense for me'—a promise that was completely against his conscience. He therefore told the master that he would prefer to leave the college than stay on these terms. His tutor intervened on his behalf and brought the master a 'peg lower', with the hope that their 'squabble' could be settled amicably. Rowland's only prayer was that all things would be done to the glory of God and that he would keep a clear conscience.

The master replied to Rowland through his tutor that he could stay if he did not disturb the town by public meetings and promised not to teach in the university any doctrine contrary to the thirty nine Articles. Rowland agreed to the first condition, but to the second he could not agree if the master meant that he should not talk about religion to the gownsmen; but if he meant no more than the words implied, he could agree with all his heart. Once again his tutor acted as intermediary.

Rowland's desire was to be made an able minister of the New Testament, not of the letter but of the spirit. His yearning was to have 'a heart totally given up to God's service; I then know that however weak I may be in myself, God's power shall be manifested in me. I long to see myself *nothing*, and Christ *all*, to learn by experience that glorious song, *Worthy is the Lamb.*'

4. Whitefield's mantle

After his degree Rowland set his sights on obtaining orders and was confident of entering the ministry by the following May. At the thought of such an important office his heart trembled and he saw himself as 'nothing but sin, ignorance and blindness, utterly unqualified for so great an employment'. He knew that if he was to become a minister of the New Testament, he must first give himself up wholly to Christ, for it requires 'much grace simply to follow the Lamb wheresoever he goeth, to forget self, love of ease, &c. to scorn contempt and every cross, and give up all to the glory of God'.

Ordination, however, proved an obstacle that took four years to overcome. Rowland's 'methodistical ways' and his reluctance to promise to confine himself to the rules of the Church of England caused six bishops to refuse him ordination. Looking back to this uncertain time, Rowland said, 'For visiting the sick and imprisoned, and expounding the Scriptures in private houses, I met with no less than six refusals, before I gained admission into the established church—but, blessed be God, all this proved for the furtherance of the Gospel.'

One of the problems was that he continued to preach before making his applications for admission into the church, which did not sit easily with the bishops. He loved his Cambridge flock and could not leave them to 'ravenous wolves', and so went frequently to the university to feed them. He also travelled to different parts of England to preach the good news, partly driven on by an impression on his mind that he was not going to live long, so he desired to use every moment in the active service of God.

In the spring of 1770, he encountered trials and difficulties he had not before experienced. Apart from his father's displeasure and his failure to obtain orders, he met with 'violent opposition on many occasions, and was often pelted and abused by the assemblies he addressed'. Eggs and stones were thrown at him, and he was lampooned and burnt in effigy, but none of these things moved him.

Whitefield's death on 30 September that year was a great loss to Rowland and deprived him of a wise counsellor and friend. In his grief he wrote a beautiful sketch of his friend's character and success.

It pleased God to give him a most enlarged mind, and liberated him from all the wretched trammels of education. He knew no party; his glory was to preach the Gospel to every creature. Bigotry his soul abhorred...

I thank God for that permissive providence, whereby that great man, being turned out of the churches, esteemed it his duty to preach at large. His first attempt was among the poor Kingswood colliers; and I defy any missionary upon earth to find a darker spot, or to visit a more benighted people. These he called out of the holes and dens of the earth, and to these he preached 'repentance towards God, and faith in our Lord Jesus Christ'. Oh! it was a lovely sight to behold the glorious effect! Eyes unaccustomed to weep before, now began to flow with tears of repentance unto life; white streaks appearing thereby on their black faces, now turned up towards heaven, praying for mercy and forgiveness. Knees unaccustomed to prayer before, were now bent in fervent devotion before God; and their lives well and wisely regulated by the power of that grace which had done such wonders in their hearts.

Edwin Sidney was convinced that after Whitefield's death there was only one man who had 'caught the fire of his zeal, possessed similar powers of eloquence, and was actuated by the same self-denying and disinterested spirit', and that man was Rowland Hill. 'His doctrines, his preaching talents, his popularity, his want of any definite system, were all Whitefield again.' Whitefield's followers certainly flocked around Rowland, 'owned him as their leader, and acknowledged that their drooping cause was revived through his instrumentality, both in London and in various parts of the kingdom. His appearance in every place was the signal for revival.'

The Scottish Baptist, William Jones, who was not always sympathetic to Rowland, speaks along similar lines when he comments that Whitefield was Rowland's 'prototype and model in many respects, though he [Rowland] was not a slavish imitator... Mr Hill was not a whit behind

Whitefield's Tabernacle, Moorfields

Tottenham Court Road Chapel

him [Whitefield], in his laborious exertions and disinterested efforts to spread abroad a savour of the knowledge of Christ in every place.' He agrees that Whitefield's mantle fell on Rowland, who 'wore it with equal grace. The same contempt of ecclesiastical statutes ... the same fearless exposure to personal danger from the rude insults of the rabble—the same noise and vociferation in their manner of address—the same effort at wit and pleasantry ... all these were prominent features in both orators.'

It was supposed that Rowland would succeed the great preacher at the Tabernacle and Tottenham Court chapels, and some even accused him of striving 'to convert this opinion into fact, by endeavouring to place himself in the vacant seat of the departed prophet, and henceforth hold the crook of supreme pastoral authority over the flock' Whitefield had left behind. Rowland, however, was too anxious at this time for episcopal ordination to take a step that might exclude him altogether from official connection with the Church of England. He did occasionally preach at both chapels and the crowds were so great that many hundreds could not gain admission. He therefore followed in the footsteps of his predecessor and went out into the fields to compel sinners to come into God's kingdom. He went to Hampstead Heath, where the multitude first mocked his doctrines, and then many embraced them, and his labours there were greatly blessed.

Rowland usually stayed with his parents at Hawkstone for the winter, but during the other seasons of the year he preached the gospel in many other places. In the autumn of 1770, while with Buckley, many were converted under his ministry in Yorkshire, particularly at Leeds, from where Mr Iveson wrote to him later, saying, 'Many souls here remember with joy and gratitude the happy times they enjoyed under your ministry.' The writer then mentioned how John Wesley had spoken highly of his preaching in a letter to Miss Hirrold, and how the Wesleyans at Leeds 'regarded him with sincere affection, and were much attached to his preaching'.

The thrilling scenes that attended his preaching of the gospel in Yorkshire are described in an extract from one of his letters to his sister Jane:

I cannot tell you what glorious blessings we have enjoyed. Though before many blessings had been granted, yet the continued increase of the power of God, and the many thousands that attend can never be conceived by any but those who are sharers in our blessings. There is not any part into which I have been, but more or less the glory of God has cordially been revealed. Leeds has been particularly favoured: though the congregations were at first but thin, yet they have increased by thousands of a week night. A place calculated to hold full five thousand people, is now so crowded that one might walk upon their heads.

On Sundays large numbers went away for lack of room, while those that remained enjoyed 'the sweetest waterings' that ever could be wished for. Old professors were so touched that they wept uncontrollably, while whole families of children were awakened to such an extent that they spent the night agonising for the blessings of the Lord. Christians were abundantly blessed and overpowered with grace, and particularly with the spirit of supplication and thanksgiving, that they continually prayed or praised, unable to sleep in their beds for the joy of the presence of the Lord. According to Rowland, the greatest mercy was that many were 'pricked at the heart, who before knew nothing of the Lord. In short, all in Leeds bear testimony that they scarce ever remember such an outpouring of the Spirit of God.'

The last Sunday he spent in the town he thought would never be forgotten. He preached three times at a chapel a little way out of town and enjoyed such a 'love feast as was delightful to a degree'. His congregation 'were almost all at times in tears for joy, and went away only grieved that our time was so short'. For eleven hours that day, with only two hours rest, he was either praying or preaching or exhorting, and yet he had more of the power of God with him at the last than at the first, and his body was considerably strengthened.

In the spring of 1771 he started preaching in Bristol and the surrounding neighbourhood, and was introduced to the Tabernacle congregation there by Cornelius Winter, who commented, 'From the Sabbath on which I had the pleasure to introduce him into the Tabernacle pulpit, has religion been reviving through his instrumentality, and the flame has burned strong ever since.

His parents' continued disapproval of his ministry deeply saddened him and he often wept in silent agony, but he could not turn his back on the conviction in his heart to preach the gospel whenever and wherever he could. To obey their command, would have meant affluence and ease, it is true, but there was a higher calling on his life, to which he was prepared to devote himself regardless of the consequences.

In May, Berridge wrote to him with deep affection. 'I feel my heart go out towards you whilst I am writing, and can embrace you as my second self... Surely it is a pleasant thing to love with a pure heart fervently, and something of this love I feel for you, which brings a melting tear into my eye, and refreshes my very body as I write.' He then exhorted him to:

Go forth, my dear Rowley, whenever you are invited into the devil's territories; carry the Redeemer's standard along with you, and blow the Gospel trumpet boldly, fearing nothing but yourself. If you meet with success, as I trust you will, expect clamour and threats from the world, snares and grins from any professors and a little venom now and then from the children. These bitter herbs make good sauce for a young recruiting sergeant, whose heart would be lifted up with pride, if it was not kept down by these pressures. The more success you meet with, the more opposition you will find; but Jesus sitteth above the water floods and remaineth a king for ever.

With such support and encouragement, Rowland could not but feel refreshed in heart and invigorated in his ministry.

On the same day as the above letter, Berridge wrote to Lady Huntingdon and noticed Rowland's preaching at Bath. 'I find you have got honest Rowland down to Bath: he is a pretty young spaniel, fit for land or water, and has a wonderful yelp. He forsakes father and mother and brethren, and gives up all for Jesus;—and I believe will prove a useful labourer, if he keeps clear of petticoat snares.'

On 10 May Rowland was at Stowey, where he spoke to the 'most outrageous congregation' he had ever encountered. There was so much noise from beating of pans, blowing of horns and ringing of bells that he could hardly hear himself speak. He was pelted with dirt and eggs, but was enabled to finish his sermon. He moved on to Putsham and spoke out of doors to a serious and attentive congregation, some of whom were comforted in their souls. Others at a distance scoffed, while several threw stones. One man was slightly injured and another almost stunned by a blow that cut him badly over the eye. Rowland had no idea who the culprits were, so he simply wrote in his diary, 'May the Lord forgive and convert them.'

Two days later he had 'a day much to be remembered'. He preached in the morning at Putsham to a few serious people. After dinner he rode to Watchet, where he preached out of doors 'with some freedom and power' on the prodigal son to 'some hundreds, who behaved with the deepest attention'. Rowland thought the town 'totally conquered'. From there he rode to the market town of Dunster, where there was a congregation of 'near 2000 hearers'. Thanks to a magistrate who was determined to punish offenders, all opposition seemed to be at an end and the people behaved with the 'most awful attention', while he preached with much freedom. After a little refreshment he went with 300 people to Minehead, where a congregation of 2000 soon gathered. 'All but a very few of the upper sort of people behaved with remarkable attention,' wrote Rowland in his diary, 'and seemed deeply struck at the majesty of the word, which came with power, and having great liberty, and being enabled to pour forth my soul amongst them with much love.'

It was about this time (the summer of 1771) that Rowland was used by God to help the ministry of his brother Richard. Sir Rowland Hill was delighted that Richard had decided to stop 'open-air preaching, against the canons of the Church of England as he saw it', and sent him to Bristol to persuade Rowland to follow his lead and return home. On his arrival at Bristol, Richard discovered that Rowland had gone to Kingswood to preach to the colliers. He

Richard Hill

immediately followed him and found him surrounded by a huge crowd, who were listening intently to the solemn appeal he was making to their consciences.

Rowland spotted his brother in the congregation and, guessing the reasons for his attendance, continued with increased passion. Soon there were white channels of tears running down the faces of the colliers, which deeply affected Richard. Rowland, making the most of the situation, suddenly announced at the end of the service, 'Mr brother, Richard Hill, Esq., will preach here at this time tomorrow.' Taken by surprise by such an announcement, and with the impression of the meeting still lying heavily upon him, he consented; and instead of returning home with his 'obedient brother' in tow, he became his assistant in the very work he had set out to stop!

On Sunday 16 June he preached at Dursley to huge crowds, and that evening he went for the first time to Wotton-under-Edge, Gloucestershire, which was to become his favourite summer residence. An old lady from a very respectable family in the town, who was awakened under Rowland's ministry, was very fond of describing his first visit to Wotton.

She was sitting at tea, when a relation suddenly came in, and said, 'Ann, the baronet's son, who goes about preaching, is now under the market house.'

'Are you sure it is the baronet's son himself?'

'Yes, that I am, for I saw his brother, Mr Richard Hill, not long ago, and he is so like him, I am sure he is of the same family.'

Upon this she accompanied her friend out of curiosity to see and hear the stranger, little thinking of the alteration his preaching would be the means of producing in her own views of herself and of her Saviour. One man who stood by her seized a stone and was going to throw it at Mr Hill; but another who was near him laid hold of his arm and said, in the broad dialect of Gloucestershire, 'If thee dost touch him, I'll knock thy head off,' when the assailant dropped the stone, and the people all became quiet, overawed by the solemnity of the subject, and the earnestness of the preacher.

His main opponents on this tour were the people of Devizes, who pelted him with eggs and stones, and followed him to the next village, where many 'poor simple people' were longing to hear, but 'some of the Devizes persecutors spoilt the opportunity by molesting us as much as they could'. He was similarly treated at Marlborough, where he spoke on the green to a 'very rude and rebellious congregation, who laughed even at the mention of the text—they pelted me with stones and eggs, but through mercy I was not hurt'.

On one occasion in this area he preached on a village green to a large crowd, who became very wild and threw every kind of missile at him. His subject was the power of the shield of faith to quench the fiery darts of the evil one, and just as he was speaking of the attacks of Satan, one member of the crowd released a live snake into the congregation to frighten the women and interrupt the worship. Rowland bent down and quietly picked it up in his handkerchief, convincing his hearers that their fears were groundless. He placed it beneath his feet and said, 'This is one of the darts of the wicked one, but faith enables me not to fear.' His assailant was so impressed by the preacher's calm manner that he listened carefully to the remainder of the sermon. Afterwards he went up to Rowland and acknowledged his offensive behaviour, and became a devoted Christian for the rest of his life.

A more exaggerated account of this story has been passed down. According to one biographer, three snakes were thrown at Rowland. One coiled on his arm and another fastened around his neck. Rowland said,

Perceiving at once that they were harmless, I merely took them off, and threw them behind me away from the crowd in attendance; some of the people immediately drove away the sinner, and the result was increased attention and several conversions to God. Soon afterwards the rebel came again to hear me; and he that would have alarmed me by serpents, was himself rescued from the old serpent, and became for many years a steadfast follower of the Lamb of God.

What is certain is that many years after Rowland had preached in the market place at Devizes, he was the means of leading a young man to Christ, who became a minister of the gospel and who for more than thirty years successfully preached the saving grace of Jesus in that very town.

5. Growing popularity

In the summer of 1772 Rowland rode to London and preached to immense congregations at Whitefield's Tabernacle and Tottenham Court chapels, where he was one of the most popular supplies and the means of reviving the cause of Methodism. Seymour comments that his 'labours in the metropolis were immense; and great and small bore testimony to the power with which he spoke. The displays of gospel grace under the ministry of this faithful labourer in the Lord's vineyard were truly surprising; and his success was, from the beginning, as great as the situation in which he stood was peculiar and eminent.' Lady Huntingdon, in a letter written at this time, overflowed with praise towards 'this *second Whitefield*'.

Some years later, the *Evangelical Biography* also made a similar connection between Rowland and Whitefield, when it remarked, 'Becoming famous for his almost unparalleled zeal and originality, he [Rowland Hill] drew a great number of people after him. Perhaps the doctrine of Calvin had not been so vehemently enforced by any preacher from the death of the famous Mr Whitefield to this time.'

Rowland stayed at the Tabernacle house in Moorfields, from where he made his preaching excursions into the city and its neighbourhood, and the effects of these tours were extraordinary. One person wrote to him and told him how the Lord had blessed the word he had delivered to 'hundreds', even 'thousands', and pleaded with him to return as soon as possible, as 'multitudes longed for the time when they should hear him again… Many I have visited on their sick beds,' added the writer, 'blessing God for the time they heard you. Notes of thanks were put up from whole families stirred up to seek the Lord by your ministry.'

That summer he preached for the second time on Hampstead Heath on a wet day from Deuteronomy 32:2, 'My doctrine shall drop as the rain.' Towards the end of his sermon the rain became very heavy and Rowland put on his hat, and then said to the people who surrounded him, 'Excuse my hat, friends; but do not let the rain alarm us so much: what would the condemned souls in Tophet's parched pit give for a single drop of this consolatory rain, that falleth upon our delightful land, and makes fruitful our long burnt up fields.'

At that time Rowland took his MA at Cambridge and while in the neighbourhood of the university he visited his friend Berridge. In a letter to Jane Hill he explained that as he looked into the future he saw before him a scene of trials, which only God could give him grace and wisdom to surmount; but he was not inclined to turn back. 'The Lord adds his mighty blessing to my feeble labours, and I dare not stop.'

The style of Rowland's preaching at this stage in his life was simple yet forceful. It overflowed with clear views of the doctrines of the Bible, 'mingled with sudden bursts of vivid, sublime and sometimes singular illustrations'. An example of his style is found in a preface to a small work containing a sermon to those who had been converted through his ministry in London. It is dated 'Tabernacle House, 27 August 1772', and opens:

How happy is the man that can assume this character to himself—a sinner saved! Stop and consider—is it thine? O then, what miracles of mercies have been revealed to thy heart! The world by nature knows nothing of our Immanuel; but the convinced sinner knows that he is lost without him; he sees that he cannot be more completely fallen, or more certain of destruction than he is in himself. This strikes at the root of all his self righteous pride, and compels him to cry out as with the prophet of old, 'Woe is me! for I am undone.'

He now trembles at justice and prays for mercy. He sees nothing else but flaming vengeance held forth by the law; and he owns that he deserves it as his portion for his iniquities. His legal hopes from a covenant of works now fall to the ground.

Then it is the Lord the Spirit divinely convinces of the work of Jesus: he sees it, and is enabled, as his faith increases, to rest satisfied with the fulness of it; he rejoices in the dignity of it, and is happy in the security of it. This teaches him boldly to renounce all his *homespun* righteousness as dung and dross: he dares not bring it as a condition at first, or as a wretched adjunct to complete the whole at last: no; he renounces it *wholesale*, and is enabled to rest only upon Jesus as his everlasting *all*.

Chapter 5

John Wesley

Rowland took a full part in the latest round of religious controversy, which initially broke out after the minutes of the Methodist conference had been published, when it was discovered that John Wesley had made remarks that sounded as though he was supporting 'works-righteousness'. John Fletcher was Wesley's main literary defender, and Rowland and his brother Richard, along with Augustus Toplady, were his chief opponents, although many others became involved. The main point of dispute was the place of human works in the economy of God's grace, a dispute in which the Arminians were charged with legalism and the Calvinists with antinomianism. Sadly, Rowland, who was anxious to prevent any abuse of gospel grace, attacked Wesley in a way that would have shocked Whitefield and which he later regretted, saying, 'A softer style and spirit would better have become me.'

For Rowland the year 1772 was a combination of heavenly blessings and unnecessary wrangling. There was much for him to regret, but also much for him to be thankful for as he enjoyed the presence and power of God, and saw many strongholds in individual lives broken down. His reputation as a preacher was growing and in many areas his ministry was extraordinarily fruitful, but he was too quick to respond to provocation and too ready to attack personally men who disagreed with him. He was still not ordained. Being

John Fletcher

without holy orders did not perturb him unduly, but at the same time he knew ordination would increase his usefulness and open new doors for him.

6. Mary and ordination

At the beginning of 1773, while in Hawkstone, Rowland was considering two very important events—marriage and ordination. During visits to Clement Tudway, he had met and fallen in love with his sister, Mary, a truly godly woman, with whom he was going to enjoy nearly sixty years of married life. Once, when Mary was talking to William Jones, one of Rowland's biographers, she looked at her husband and said, 'Little did I think, when I first saw you at Mr—'s party, that you would ever be my husband; you appeared unhappy all the evening, stood alone, and seemed to be something quite out of place.' Rowland responded with a gentle smile.

Probably the first letter Rowland wrote to Mary Tudway was written from London just before he left the metropolis to go to Cambridge to take his MA. In the letter he unveiled his true feelings: 'I think I can safely say with all my heart, as before the presence of God, that I love your person.' He was also fully persuaded of a true work of grace on her soul, although she herself occasionally doubted what God had done. He then asked her to marry him, 'Thus, as a man and as a Christian, with your leave, would I be glad to make choice of you as my partner through life.' He next set out, as honestly as he could, what he thought life would be like for her married to a 'poor worm in the character of a minister of Christ'.

The present plan of labour ... will frequently compel me to leave my home ... and to take up at times the life of an itinerant, and such a life as this you must expect will sometimes be attended, as to myself, with hardships and contempt. Were your kindness for my person, however it might be the language of love, to make you attempt to dissuade me from this, such dissuasion would not only be a burden upon my mind, but also, if not complied with, a grief to yourself... Do you think you could make your mind perfectly easy in thus giving me up to the service of the Lord? Can you be contented to see me a despised pilgrim for my once despised master, rejected for my labours, and reproached for my God?

He reaffirmed his love for her and said, 'I shall always think it my pleasure and duty to make your life a happiness to itself… I do not request, though I shall wait with earnestness, for a speedy answer to this. Dear madam, take your time, pray it over, and if you can write, write all that is in your mind.'

Clement Tudway was instrumental in helping to get Rowland ordained deacon, a kindness that Rowland noted in a letter to Mary dated 2 February 1773 and written at the home of Thomas Powys of Berwick, Shropshire. After mentioning that he did not arrive home until the previous Friday, having been stopped on Thursday on the road 'by the severest wetting' he had ever experienced, and that his long stay away from home had not been mentioned by his parents, he proceeded to thank Tudway, who was willing to apply to his 'old bishop for ordination'. 'So far as I can,' wrote Rowland, 'without wounding my conscience, I would do the utmost in my power not to frustrate the event.' He was even prepared to withdraw for a time from 'more public labours, so as not to give immediate disgust', if there was a probability of success. However, he could not think of giving any future promises of altering his conduct from what it was at present, even after his ordination, if he felt it was right to go on as before.

He then listed a few 'hints' for Tudway to consider in his application.

It might be represented that I am a younger brother with a small fortune, that I was *bred up for the Church*, have taken two degrees, consequently much has been expended on my education; but that all is lost upon me without ordination—and that it is now too late to turn my hands to any other employment in life, &c. &c. &c.—and if he (the bishop) has heard of all my doings, it might be mentioned to him that, as I have taken a *religious turn*, it might be much better to ordain me, and let me into the Church, *than to compel me to go preaching in the fields, whether I would or no.*

If his lordship took time to consider his application, Rowland was quite happy in the interval to get proper testimonials, title and whatever else was needed.

If, however, the bishop appeared reluctant, Tudway was to explain that Rowland only needed deacon's orders, as the bishop of Carlisle had promised second orders whenever he applied. The reason for this was that Rowland had been turned down by the bishop of Ely, and the bishop of Carlisle, who had only just come on the bench, was unwilling to counteract the bishop of Ely, but said that after he was ordained deacon, he would immediately ordain him priest.

In the whole matter of ordination Rowland was happy to leave it to the Lord and to 'preserve a conscience spotless in the affair'. He would be thankful for ordination, but only according to God's will. He was also delighted that Mary Tudway wanted him to keep an 'honest conscience before God, than by in the least injuring it, to enjoy the greatest advantages that this world can give'.

In between this letter and Rowland's proposal of marriage, Mary had agreed to the union, which spurred Rowland on to make all the necessary preparations, including trying to buy a house in Bristol. 'I cannot help frequently making you the subject of my prayers,' he wrote to his beloved. 'You are to be united to one who must bear the cross—this makes me feel for you with a tenderness and sympathy I cannot express.'

Mary replied to Rowland's 2 February letter as soon as she arrived in London and mentioned that she lacked the assurance of salvation, fearing she was a hypocrite. Rowland, who had no such fears about her spiritual state, wrote to her again and tried to reassure her that they had a 'faithful, unchangeable, covenant keeping God in Christ, as our God of grace, to preserve us safe in our journey from time to eternity'. He gently reproved her for speaking the language of unbelief and for looking too much into herself, where 'all is misery'. He then offered the solution to her doubts: 'Look but to Jesus, and there is salvation in abundance… Remember this, that Mary Tudway is as bad as she can be—she is utterly undone—now where is she to look? Only to Jesus. Her vile heart never can withstand the power of his grace. Has she millions of sins that threaten her destruction? The Lord has received double for them all. In Jesus she is complete.'

Hawkstone, from where he wrote to Mary, was a 'furnace' of trials for him at this time. The previous Sunday his father had forbidden him to leave the family to preach at Hardwick, which, along with waiting for news from his brother about ordination, was making his present situation feel like 'nothing but idleness, and almost total loss of time'—a situation that hurt his conscience 'not a little'. He was afraid that the attempts for ordination would keep him from his work, which he was fully persuaded was God's call on his life.

On Wednesday 24 March, Rowland ran out of patience and left home on a short preaching journey. Mary feared that his irregularities, if they became known, would prove an obstacle to his ordination and advised him to stop. In reply, which was written from Woburn, Rowland, although he wanted to go to Cambridge, thought it better not to go as he was so well known there and would receive many invitations to preach. He decided to stay at Woburn until the bishop's answer was received, which he hoped would be on Saturday at the latest.

With an increasing likelihood of a favourable answer from the bishop he retired reluctantly into Shropshire, and preached a few sermons at places like Hardwick and Marchamley. As has already been intimated, it was virtually impossible for him not to preach—preaching was his life; so much so that when he was older, his wife used to say frequently, 'What I dread is, lest he should ever be so feeble as not to be able to preach—in that case, what would become of him I cannot tell.'

In a letter to Mary he told her that he was giving up the house at Bristol and that a house was being built for him at Wotton-under-Edge in a spot of singular beauty. Opposite the house was a 'perfect amphitheatre of hill', most of which was clothed with a hanging wood. From the top of a hill to the left of the house there was a stunning landscape: the Welsh mountains, the Malvern Hills, the green vale of Berkeley, the River Severn, and a foreground of grassy knolls and trees could all be enjoyed. In front of the house was a winding rocky path that ran through a wood of beech trees. Not surprisingly, it soon became for him 'the spot I love'.

The Tabernacle at Wotton was built soon after Rowland's ordination to deacon's orders. It was capable of seating about 700 persons and was described, somewhat harshly, as 'mean in its external appearance, and inconvenient in its internal arrangements'. One of its curious features was

Rowland Hill setting out from his house

the 'absence of a vestry. The deacons meet the minister in the manse, and then pass up a semi-subterranean staircase through a door in the wall, and enter the tabernacle behind the pulpit.' On Sundays 'the approaching road teemed with human beings ... coming to hear the word from the lips of their beloved minister', who, unbeknown to them, was watching them through a telescope from his bedroom window! If he detected any frivolous or unseemly behaviour, there was sure to be an allusion to it in the sermon. 'We must mind what we do,' was the general comment, 'for Master Hill knows everything, bless him.'

Once, when Lord Hill was a guest at Wotton and William Jay was also visiting his friend, an amusing incident occurred.

Rowland Hill was called out of the room by his servant. It appears that one of the managers of his chapel, by trade a dyer, a little man, called on him in his working dress, besmeared with blue, about the chapel arrangements. This business settled, Mr Hill said, 'I should like, my good friend, to introduce you to my nephew, the great

Rowland Hill's house and chapel at Wotton

general.' Upon which the little dyer replied, 'Look, respected sir, at my hands and clothes; I should be ashamed to face him.' No sooner was the sentence finished than Rowland Hill, without more ado, caught hold of the dyer's hands, slapped him on the back, and brought him into the room, then letting him down, said to his nephew, 'There is my deacon; and I can assure you that he is one of the best of men living.' Lord Hill, like a true gentleman, took particular notice of the dyer, and made various inquiries of him about his trade.

On 23 May 1773 Rowland and Mary were married at Mary le bone Church, and they started a long and happy life together, although they had no children. Berridge for one said how much he liked Mary when they met in London and often sent his kind love to her. William Jay called her a

...very excellent female. She was a truly gracious woman, of a very sound understanding, and possessing the ornament of a meek and quiet spirit, which is in the sight of God of great price. She was formed for a minister's wife by her prudence, peaceableness, untalkative temper, and unintermeddling conduct. She was singularly suited to the man she espoused; and our friend's obligations to those properties in her character which tended to qualify the peculiarities of his own, were great.

Many untrue stories were subsequently told of Rowland's carelessness as a husband and of his public allusions to his wife, most of which he found amusing, simply commenting, 'I wonder at people's invention.' Once, however, when told it had been reported that he had made some remarks in public on his wife's dress, he exclaimed angrily, 'It is an abominable untruth—derogatory to my character as a Christian and a gentleman: they would make me out a bear.' On another occasion, when he heard of a slanderous report, he exclaimed, 'I will so live that nobody will believe it.' Similarly, his indignation was aroused when he referred to some who had given currency to certain baseless stories about him, 'I have humbled myself in following these gentry in language almost as low as their own; like eels, they are now at liberty to sink into their own mud and dirt as their safest place of refuge.'

Immediately after their wedding they went into Somerset, where Rowland was ordained deacon by Dr Wills, the aged bishop of Bath and Wells, on Trinity Sunday (6 June). His title to orders was the parish of Kingston, which was about four miles from Taunton, Somerset, and where he stayed for about a year. His ordination, much to his relief and satisfaction, was *without any promise or condition whatever*, and his stipend was £40 a year.

He was long remembered by the people of Kingston and several stories about him were handed down from one generation to the next. On one occasion he deeply offended the farmers by saying they were as bad as their pigs. Later, when several of them were together in a house at the bottom of the village, they saw Rowland pass by. They called him in and demanded an explanation of his comment, which he immediately gave.

Now, [said Rowland], look at your pigs; when the acorns drop, they do not go under the elm in search of them, but under the oak; and when they have swallowed all they can find, off they go, without giving a single look at the tree which has furnished their meal. So you, like your pigs, know where to go to look for your wheat, and other produce; and when your barns are filled with plenty, like them, you forget to look up to the Source whence all your blessings have been obtained.

The farmers appreciated Rowland's frankness, although they did not care much for the comparison!

On another occasion the farmers complained that Rowland ranted so loudly that he could be heard throughout the village. Rowland referred to these remarks from the pulpit, and with deep feeling exclaimed, while pointing to a sleeping farmer, 'What! Shall we not lift up our voice like a trumpet, and cry aloud, and spare not, when, with all our ranting, sinners can sleep, and be damned under our very sermons?' The old farmer was jolted out of his sleep and heard the last remark. He quickly rose from his pew, left the church and declared he would never enter it again—a promise he stubbornly kept for the rest of his life.

It was probably during this period that he spoke in the open air at a seaport town and was 'so interrupted by noise and missiles' that it was impossible for him to continue. He stopped preaching and addressed the crowd with these words:

My lads, I have no right over you; if you do not chose to hear me, I have no authority to force your attention; but I have travelled some miles for the sake of doing or receiving good; I have, therefore, a proposal to make to you. I always did admire British sailors. I see here some able-bodied seamen: some of you, no doubt, have seen a great deal of service, and been in many a storm, and some in dangerous shipwrecks. Now, as I am very fond of hearing the adventures of seamen, my proposal is, that some of you, and, as many as you please in turn, shall stand up, and tell us what you have seen and suffered, and what dangers you have escaped; and I will sit and hear you out, upon this condition: that you agree to hear me afterwards.

Such a proposal made many of them snigger and they said to one another, 'Do you stand up, and give us a lecture.' One called to a talkative sailor by name, 'I say, Harry, do you give him a lecture,' which caused a loud burst of laughter throughout the crowd. Rowland, to keep them in good humour, laughed with them. After waiting some time, Rowland said, 'Will none of you take up my proposal?' As none responded, he said, 'I am a clergyman. I came, not long since, from the University of Cambridge. If you had heard me, I should have told you nothing but what is in the Bible or Prayer Book. I will tell you what I intended to say to you, if you had heard me quietly.'

And then beginning with a declaration of the grace and compassion of Christ, in dying to save all penitent sinners, he led them to the consideration of the thief on the cross; and then to the character and circumstances of the prodigal son, and the compassion of his father. His description of what he meant to have said was so interesting and affecting, that he riveted their attention, and produced an evident change in their disposition towards him. While he was speaking they drew gradually nearer, hanging, as is the practice of sailors, when standing in a crowd, upon each others' shoulders. In this position they listened, with almost death-like silence, till he had finished telling them what he should have said, if they had been willing to hear him. He then took off his hat, made them bow, and thanked them for their civilities. Most of them took off their hats, and gave him three cheers: several vociferated, 'When will you come again, Sir?' And one man, who seemed like the champion of the whole, approached Mr Hill, and said, 'If you come again, Sir, I say no one shall hurt a hair of your head, if I am on shore.' Mr Hill promised that he would visit them again, as soon as other engagements would permit. There are now [1833], in that town and neighbourhood, several places of worship; and it is as quiet and orderly a seaport as any in the kingdom.

In the neighbouring parish to Kingston a young woman was living with her uncle and aunt. She heard a great deal about Rowland and so decided to go and hear him preach. The word struck her heart with power, but, for some time, she was 'alarmed rather than convinced'. Her friends were opposed to evangelical truth and when they discovered the effects produced on her mind did all they could to prevent her from going to church. However, she managed to slip away and after hearing the sermon she felt she was 'an unpardoned sinner'. She quickly returned home and hurried into an orchard, where she fell on her knees and cried out for mercy—a spot that became very special to several of her relatives. Later she married and had nine children, who were brought up to fear the Lord, and one of her sons became a preacher.

Remembering the promise of the bishop of Carlisle that he would ordain him priest, Rowland obtained a letter dimissory from the bishop of Bath and Wells. However, the bishop of Carlisle said he had 'received an order from the archbishop of his province not to admit him to a further grade in the church, on account of his perpetual irregularity, and that he considered himself bound to obey it'. Rowland was not overly disappointed, saying somewhat philosophically, 'I thought it was my duty again to begin my public labours as usual,' which he did in earnest in London and its vicinity. So Rowland passed through life 'wearing only one ecclesiastical boot'. But if one door closed, another opened, for in September 1773 he was appointed chaplain to Melusina, Countess Dowager of Chesterfield.

Rowland was deeply grieved by the death of his mother on Friday 17 December. The first text he preached from after her death was 2 Samuel 23:5: 'Although my house be not so with God, yet he hath made with me an everlasting covenant, ordered in all things and sure.' His hearers at the Tabernacle recognised the allusion to his mother, who had strongly opposed the course he was pursuing.

In many ways, his sermon on this occasion summed up his ministry, because he usually chose the subject that was nearest to his heart at the time, and spoke on it in a lively and fresh manner. Sheridan said of him, 'I go to hear Rowland Hill because his ideas come red hot from the heart.' After one sermon in which he had given full vent to his feelings and experience on the Christian's joy, Ambrose Serle, an under-secretary to Lord Dartmouth, rushed into the vestry at Surrey Chapel, grabbed him by the hand and exclaimed, 'Oh, my dear sir, if we are so happy now, what shall we be a hundred thousand years hence in heaven?' On another occasion, Dr Milner, the dean of Carlisle, was so moved by one of his sermons that he went to him and said, 'Mr Hill, Mr Hill, I *felt* today—'tis this *slap dash* preaching, say what they will, that does all the good.'

After his marriage, Mary Hill, who appears only to have been well known in her own immediate circle, accompanied him on most of his preaching expeditions. She neither complained about the hardship she had to endure, nor placed any obstacles in the path of her husband's duty to God, although she did try to discourage him from doing those things that might damage his health. She rejoiced in his spiritual prosperity and was anxious he should always abound in the work of the Lord. After Rowland inherited a fortune, which enabled him to be very generous, she would sometimes 'gently but prudently pull the curb, knowing that he would give away his last shilling with joy, without remembering the just claims of his own household'. Mary was the 'faithful chronicler of his engagements, which she always recorded in an interleaved copy of an almanack'.

7. 'Blessed effects'

In 1774 Rowland preached charity sermons in many London churches, where the 'church wardens and overseers turned Methodists *pro tempore*' and saw their collection plates filled with the contributions of Rowland's followers. He was often at St John's, Wapping, and there occasionally gave way to an offensive humour, which he afterwards regretted. On one of these occasions, noticing that his large congregation was made up of 'seafaring persons, who were not celebrated for overmuch religion', he remarked, 'I am come to preach to great sinners, notorious sinners, profane sinners,' adding with peculiar emphasis, 'yea, to *Wapping* sinners.' This last remark 'operated like an electric shock through all the congregation' and some were highly offended, who felt themselves 'insulted by such a debasement of their place of abode'.

At this time he made many preaching excursions to Richmond, where he endured violent opposition. On one occasion an attempt was made to persuade him not to go to Richmond as a party of young men had hired a boat and were sailing down the river determined to pull him through the water; but an invisible hand protected him, for he was soon informed that the boat had capsized and all its occupants drowned.

He spent a short time in Bristol and then, on his way into Wales, he preached at a 'blessed consecration of an old barn in the morning'. At this time he was in the habit of preaching in the open air at what he called 'field campaigns'. He used to go into large towns on market days and preach to the crowds in the market houses. When he heard about a fair or a revel in a certain place he went there to preach, in spite of the violence that was often directed at him. His favourite text on such occasions was 'Come out from among them,' which he applied so forcefully to the consciences of his hearers, that some of them, convinced of their wicked life, hurried home to repent. Many were converted after his solemn warnings to them, even though they stood in the midst of a riotous mob.

Throughout his tour of Wales he preached three or four times a day, and each sermon was at least an hour long. Thousands of Welsh men and women followed him from one place to another and nothing could stop them from attending. Many times he stood in the pouring rain preaching to a huge crowd, who were unconcerned at the drenching they were receiving, which he often mentioned to the English, when bad weather kept them at home on the Sabbath. 'If you loved the gospel as the Welsh do, you would not mind a shower.' However, he could not tolerate the Welsh 'jumpers', as they were known, commenting, 'I like the fire; but don't like the smoke.'

While on his travels he was not forgotten by his London friends, who kept him informed about the condition of his hearers in the metropolis. Captain Joss wrote him a long letter about how his last visit had been remarkably blessed. Emmanuel's 'word runs and is glorified'. Many had been awakened and several of them had joined the society. Joss then related an instance that he had heard first hand.

Captain Torial Joss

A young lady came to hear you out of curiosity, when it pleased the Lord to call her, I believe savingly. She was greatly persecuted by an elder brother, who was head of the family, as the mother is a widow: however, by her patience and conversation she was made the means of the conversion of a sister, and that sister of another, and she of the conversion of the aged mother; and who knows but the Lord may save the brother also? Thus the Lord gives them you by clusters: no wonder you meet with so much ballast; you would overset without it.

After 'in some measure, a happy ramble through Wales', Rowland returned to Wotton and revisited, day after day, all the scenes of his former labours in Gloucestershire. At Wotton, he enjoyed a peaceful haven and many of his sermons were full of illustrations from the countryside around him. On one occasion he was preaching in the afternoon, 'the only time when it seemed possible to be drowsy under him', according to William Jay, when he spotted some of the congregation sleeping. He paused saying, 'I have heard that the miller can sleep while the mill is going, but if it stops it awakens him. I'll try this method.' He duly sat down and before long the sleepers in the congregation were aroused.

At this time he preached every day wherever he could gather a congregation, whether it be in churches, chapels, fields, gardens or the streets. He found particular satisfaction in occupying pulpits in the church and reacted sensitively when he was excluded from them.

Sometimes the courage he showed awed his most violent opponents and on one occasion caused two or three highwaymen to run for their lives. He was travelling with his wife in a horse drawn carriage somewhere near London, when two or three men stopped them in the dark and aggressively demanded their money. These men, one of whom was Will Crewe, the notorious Cotswold highwayman, had only just attacked Rowland's assistant Mr Whitefoot, who preceded him in a gig. When they approached Rowland, he appeared at the window and gave such a 'tremendous unearthly shout', that one of the robbers cried out, 'We have stopped the devil by mistake, and had better be off,' and with that they disappeared into the night. When retelling this story Rowland used to laugh heartily and say, 'I stood up in the carriage and made all the outrageous noises I could think of, which frightened the fellows out of their wits, and away they scampered.'

Rowland delighted in the consistent lives and zealous devotion of many of his converts at Wotton. One of them named Rugg, lived such a godly and useful life that even his enemies admired and were awed by his character. His pastor used to refer to him as 'one of the most complete Christians he ever met with'. The reason for mentioning him here is because of his connection with the following story about the highwayman Will Crewe. After the attempted robbery referred to above, Rowland, as an act of mercy and in the hope of plucking a brand from the fire, employed Will Crewe as his gardener. He then passed him onto a friend at Trowbridge, where he attended the chapel and became, supposedly, a reformed character under the influence of religion. Soon several burglaries and other daring robberies occurred in the neighbourhood. Even the chapel was broken into and the silver communion cups and poor-box money stolen. Until Crewe was caught in the act, no one had suspected him of any wrongdoing. He and his companions, as masked highwaymen, were eventually overpowered. Crewe was tried at Gloucester, condemned and executed.

Before the sentence was carried out Rowland visited him in gaol and during their conversations he confessed the many crimes he had committed. During one of the interviews, Rowland asked,

'How was it, William, that you never robbed me, when you have had such abundant opportunity?'

'Sir,' replied he, 'do you recollect the juniper bush on the border against the dining room? I have many times hid under it at night, intending, which I could easily have done, to get into the house and plunder it—but, sir, I was afraid; something said to me, he is a man of God, it is a house of prayer—if I break in there I shall surely be found out—so I never could pluck up courage to attempt it.'

In another conversation, Crewe said,

Sir, I well knew that old Mr Rugg was in the habit of carrying a deal of money in his pocket; times and times have I hid behind the hedge of the lane leading to his house— he has passed within a yard of me, when going home from the prayer meeting, again and again—I could not stir—I durst not touch so holy a man. I was afraid. I always began trembling as soon as he came near me, and gave up the thought altogether, for I knew he was a holy man.

On the day of execution, 10,000 people gathered around the gallows, where several criminals were to be hanged. Crewe was allowed to speak and declared that there was no real pleasure in the life he had lived.

He exhorted the people to keep the Sabbath and attend God's House, and prayed that the shadow of his sin might not be disastrous to his relatives and descendants.

With his closing words as though inspired to deliver a Divine message, and as the bodies dangled in the air, came from the black clouds overhead blinding flashes of lightning and crashing peals of thunder that sent a shiver through the crowds and added solemnity to the awful scene.

Rowland thought the above incident gave rise to the famous but false story of how he was stopped by 'another highwayman', who was allegedly overpowered by Christian kindness and who afterwards became his coachman. Occasionally his worthy and honest coachman was annoyed by the audible whisper, 'Look! Look, there is Rowland Hill's carriage, and that is the highwayman he made his servant!' When Rowland heard this he laughed, and said, 'What *swallows* people must have, to credit such stories!' The truth is that Rowland was greatly blessed by many servants, including his coachman, who regarded his interests as their own.

Occasionally during this time he preached at Kingston, his curacy, but there is no certain record of when he finally left. When visiting that place many years later he was deeply touched when he met several old people, who told him that his youthful ministry had been the means of their salvation and that they were carrying to their graves the principles he had instilled into them all those years ago.

In London, Rowland preached in various places of worship and expounded the word during family devotional times, occasionally visiting the home of Lord Robert Manners for this purpose. He also received good news about the effects of his ministry. One individual from Bideford, who had been a notorious opponent of the truth, was wonderfully converted. 'Indeed, sir,' wrote the person who informed him, 'there seems to be a lasting impression left on the minds of many; and as for Mr—, the man I before mentioned, it does my soul good to converse with him; and the order of his house is turned upside down, from a prayerless family to a praying one.' From Northampton, Ryland sent him a long letter with a list of the people converted under his ministry in that place during three visits, with comments on their cases and progress in religion. He ended his letter by saying, 'We have vast reason to be thankful that God blessed you so gloriously among us: and

I hope the Lord will make it a means of endearing Northampton to you, and of inducing you to visit us oftener.'

On 25 November 1775, Richard Hill wrote from Hawkstone to one of his brothers, and stated the blessed effects of Rowland's ministry at Wotton and the neighbourhood.

I have seen the work and power and presence of God manifested in a wonderful manner indeed, through his instrumentality, among all sorts of people, with several of whom I have conversed, and find they have been wrought upon in a sound, rational scriptural manner. One poor man, upon whose heart God was pleased to work through my brother's preaching, sent to desire to see him whilst I was there; and I went with him to the house. We found the man in bed and past all hopes of recovery. Rowland asked him if he was afraid to die. He said, 'No, that he knew God had loved him with an everlasting love, that he had called him by his Spirit, that he had freely pardoned all his sins, and that there was no condemnation for him. I know,' he said, 'that Christ hath taken out the sting of death; in spite of all my sins, death cannot hurt me. I no more fear death than I do a visit from a Christian friend. I no more fear going into eternity, than I fear going into the next room.'

After prayer, Rowland said, 'Well, Thomas, God be with you—if we don't meet again in this world, I trust we shall meet in heaven.'

'Ay, sir,' replied he, with an effusion of tears of joy, 'I know that very well; but I have the advantage over you, for I shall be there first. Satan has been shooting at me, but I tell him he may as well let me alone, for Christ will never suffer him to hurt me.'

What a testimony is this to the reality of the religion of the blessed Jesus, and what encouragement do such facts afford us to be continually living upon him and to him and for him, knowing that our labour shall 'not be in vain in the Lord'.

On occasions he received letters from individuals convicted of harbouring unkind thoughts concerning his motives or of using abusive expressions about him. One of them said,

I most ardently, most zealously, most sincerely ask your pardon for the many unknown offences towards you, for the opprobrious and scurrilous language, for the most bitter invectives with which I have treated your name and person, and for the trouble I give you in this my prolix epistle; and likewise beg of you, in the name of the Holy One of Israel, to offer up your prayers for me, if you can possibly think me worthy; and in requital for so great a blessing you shall possess mine, not only with my lips, but with my heart.

Sometimes when he entered the pulpit, notices were squeezed into his hands containing similar words of repentance and asking if public confession might be made to that effect. At other times slips of paper were given to him just before he preached, with instances of conversions or of awful judgements so that he might make allusion to them in his sermons. Several of these notices were kept by him and labelled, 'Notices given me in the pulpit.' One of them read:

Dear Sir, for your encouragement I send you this, not to exalt you, but to lay you low at the feet of Christ Jesus. A man of a small fortune married a young woman with a little money. In a few years, through their extravagance, they spent all they had, which drove him to such ways which made him a terror to his wife and father in law, the latter of which he was determined to murder, and he set out last summer on a Sunday with a full determination to do it. Going across White Conduit Fields while you were preaching, he stopped to hear you, and the Lord pleased to send the word home with power, and it entered into his very soul, and the lion became a lamb from that very moment. The Lord showed him what a devil he was; so that his heart of stone became a heart of flesh, and he is now become the best of husbands, the best of fathers, and the best of sons in law; and as he was a terror to the neighbourhood, he is now become a wonder to all, and his father in law says he must be *in a trance*. I only send you this account, which you may indeed depend upon, and may the Lord encourage you still to go on—Amen. Be clothed with humility.

When these notices were given to him, he generally read them aloud. Once a cheeky man put a piece of paper on the reading desk, just before he read prayers. Rowland picked it up and began: 'The prayers of this congregation are desired [he then paused, before saying], well, I suppose I must finish what I have begun—*for the Rev. Rowland Hill, that he will not go riding about in his carriage on a Sunday!*' Without the slightest hesitation, he looked up calmly and said, 'If the writer of this piece of folly and impertinence is in the congregation, and will go into the vestry after service, and let me put a saddle on his back, I will ride him home instead of going in my carriage.' He then continued with the service as if nothing had happened. Sidney once told him the story and asked if it was true. He replied, 'Aye, that it is, true enough—you know I could not call him a *donkey* in the plain terms out of the reading desk.'

For these two years Rowland ministered in the power of the Spirit and many were dramatically converted under his preaching. It seems that wherever he went, God owned his labours and caused them to bear fruit. With such wonderful results of his ministry, it is hardly surprising that Jackson, writing in 1833, said, 'Perhaps no man in modern times has been more honoured than Mr Hill, as the instrument of converting souls; his talent appeared more particularly in awakening the careless, instances of which the writer has had many opportunities of witnessing, and he does not remember ever having stayed two days with Mr Hill in any town without meeting with one person or more to whom his ministry had been made useful.'

8. Battles of his own making

In September 1776 Rowland went to the anniversary services at Trevecca, which began on a Tuesday, when Davies, a Welsh clergyman, preached with great effect mostly in Welsh from Psalm 62:1. The following day, when Augustus Toplady was praying, the 'scaffolding on which he stood, with about forty ministers, students and preachers, gave way, and with one crush fell to the ground. The congregation remained very quiet, and Mr Toplady in a few minutes was providentially enabled to exclaim, "Nobody is materially hurt; this incident shall not interrupt us."' He moved to the steps of the scaffold that were still in one piece and preached a sermon from Malachi 3:17, which provided Rowland with 'the original hint of some remarkable illustrations'. The number who attended the anniversary was about 3000. Although Lady Huntingdon was in charge of the proceedings, Rowland was not asked to take part, which may have rankled him, for from about this time their relationship was not as warm or close. He never spoke of the matter, but it is evident there was uneasiness between them.

Augustus Toplady

At this period in his life Rowland started to mix politics with his sermons and to denounce, everywhere he went, the war with America, and with such 'violent language' that many noticed his change of emphasis. It undoubtedly reduced his usefulness and brought him into discredit with persons of influence.

It also made his controversy with the Wesleyans 'partly political and partly theological', and caused serious harm to his reputation and gospel aims.

Following the example of his late friend James Rouquet, he visited jails at Bristol and London, where he preached to the prisoners in such a way that seemed to gain the confidence of even the most hardened.

He maintained, while conversing with condemned criminals, a solemn dignity of manner, with an admirable control over his feelings; but when he left the cell of darkness and misery, a painful re action took place in his mind. After coming from Newgate, in London, where he had visited some poor wretch who was going to suffer death, he would scarcely eat anything at dinner, and at its conclusion drew back in his chair to the wall near the window, quite absorbed in the solemn recollection of the scene of distress. If asked a question, he answered it in an absent manner, and every now and then muttered some indistinct expression, in reference to the painful subject which had taken such a hold of his benevolent and sensitive mind.

On many occasions he returned from a lonely prison cell depressed, particularly because the impressions produced on the minds of the prisoners appeared at times to be permanent, but were all too often like the 'morning cloud and the early dew' and soon passed away. All that he wrote on the subject was felt and experienced by him and drawn with vivid colours. Sometimes he seemed to contrast his own situation with that of the prisoner's, remarking in a solemn whisper, 'O my God, what a mercy to be kept from sin by the restraining grace of thy Holy Spirit.'

Throughout 1777 he divided his time between Bristol, Wotton and London, and preached probably as many sermons as in any year of his life. He also continued to cross swords with John Wesley, whose name to him, says Luke Tyerman, 'was what a scarlet cloak is to an infuriated bull'. The latest round started when Wesley laid the foundation stone of the City Road Chapel in London, and delivered a sermon that many considered derogatory to the reputation of George Whitefield. Rowland for one was not about to let Wesley 'lay claim to the éclat of setting the first example' of field preaching, among other things. Wesley in his address gave a history of the rise and progress of Methodism, stating that Whitefield, by talking with dissenters, 'contracted strong prejudices against the Church', which led him to separate himself from Wesley and his brother.

Rowland, no doubt still smarting from his previous encounter with Wesley, took offence and immediately went on the attack. He published a 40 page pamphlet (written on 15 May 1777) entitled *Imposture Detected, and the Dead Vindicated; in a Letter to a Friend: containing some gentle Strictures on the false and libellous Harangue, lately delivered by Mr John Wesley, upon his laying the first stone of his new Dissenting meeting house, near the City Road*. His comments, however, were far from 'gentle' and far from defensible, as he himself afterwards acknowledged. He should have first submitted the draft manuscript to his elder brother Richard, who would have edited it unsparingly and made it fit for the press. When the pamphlet was eventually sent to Richard he crossed out several paragraphs, but it was too late to stop the publication. Predictably Rowland's attack stirred up an unsavoury 'pamphlet war' between two antagonistic parties.

Rowland was also upset because Wesley had criticized his political preaching and denounced his comments on the rights of the colonies as disloyal. Rowland responded strongly and declared that he and his hearers were daily praying for blessings on the king, peace on the kingdom, and wishing, as far as they could, to live at peace with all men. 'From the pulpit and the press,' he said, 'our characters are bespattered, and our sentiments most grossly misrepresented', which is precisely what he had done to Wesley. It is to be regretted that Rowland, instead of preaching nothing but the glorious gospel, used his energies to fight an unnecessary and mainly fruitless battle in such an unchristian temper.

Rowland never felt intimidated by the Countess of Huntingdon because of her position in society and was therefore less likely to pay her the respect she deserved. Sidney suggests, albeit without much basis as far as their early relationship is concerned, that he was 'not one of her ladyship's most cordial admirers. The mode in which she exercised her authority was not suited to a mind impatient of restraint.' Whatever the truth of this statement, it is apparent that the countess had treated him with great kindness, especially when he had been under the frowns of his family. 'He was as my own son received into my house, preached in my pulpits, and, as far as I know, a single offence he never had given him.'

Early in 1779 the countess took over Northampton Chapel and on 28 March of that year reopened it for public worship under its new name of Spa Fields Chapel. When it was officially registered as a dissenting meeting house three years later, many of her preacher friends felt unable to support her. According to Faith Cook, Rowland 'acted in a far from helpful manner. First he intensified the misgivings among the Welsh Calvinistic Methodist churches about the countess's decision, making it far less likely that any of their preachers would support her or preach among the Connexion chapels'. Second he opposed her party by 'attacking them with wit and sarcasm, and holding the countess up to [public] ridicule'. The former, said Lady Huntingdon, 'though not fair or upright, I should have so far despised, as for peace's sake to have passed over; but the worm that still lies at the bottom of the gourd, is his taking us all up into the pulpit, as his merry Andrews, and, through his evil jokes, leaving a bitter sting behind.'

Rowland tried to make peace by various means, but in the summer of 1781, the countess was still suspicious of his motives, 'He has been in London to offer peace; and wanted to preach in our large congregations, and by getting in bring nothing but division—but I have avoided this.' A friend wrote to Lady Huntingdon in an attempt to bring about a reconciliation:

I have now seen that Scripture fulfilled—when a person's ways please the Lord, he maketh their enemies to be at peace with them. I have been talking with two of your Ladyship's principal ones, and I find them wishing to be your very humble servants. Mr Hill is one. He says he will preach in the great Spafields chapel, if your Ladyship will give him leave. The committee have been told of it, and they are well pleased, if you will but approve him. Mr Keene says that he hopes your Ladyship will take them into favour again, and the Lord will make but one family of us all. He says it is his heart's desire to have your favour and friendship renewed. Indeed I believe that there is none of them happy without you. I hope the Lord will incline your heart to make peace.

The countess, however, was not so easily pacified. She wrote back in July, 'Without reserve to you, my kind friend, and with every best wish to dear Mr Venn, Mr Hill CANNOT preach *for me*. This must not be pressed. When we meet, I shall explain fully my present reasons. Should any future day prove it expedient, it may be considered, but be assured it cannot be NOW.' Even in her will the countess reiterated her determination to keep Rowland from preaching in her chapels.

An additional problem between these two strong characters arose when Rowland intervened in the affairs of two congregations brought into being by Trevecca students and financed by the countess. She accused him of 'trying to divide my friends from me', and of influencing them in such a way that would 'bring disgrace upon us all'. It is not clear exactly what Rowland did, but the situation 'half broke' Lady Huntingdon's heart. She told the committee at Spa Fields that as long as she lived, Rowland must never preach there again. With these various troubles, Rowland and the countess never again enjoyed the trust and intimacy they had once shared.

9. A chapel built

Several rich London businessmen were deeply affected by Rowland's preaching and as a result were eager to support him in a permanent place of worship. Rowland had often preached in the open air to huge congregations in St George's Fields, and during the Gordon riots of 1780 he spoke to assemblies of nearly 20,000 on 'righteousness, temperance and judgement to come'. Many were so touched by his preaching 'that they returned home to seek in retirement mercy from God, forgetting political excitement in the all absorbing anxiety for the salvation of their souls'.

After much prayer for divine guidance, Rowland and his friends thought St George's Fields, one of the most deprived districts of London, would be an ideal location to build a place of worship, and at length they decided to erect a building for that purpose and to call it Surrey Chapel. Rowland found many supporters who were not only willing to contribute towards the project, but to let him spend the summer months either travelling or at his home in Wotton, happy to let him appoint supply preachers to feed the flock during his absence.

John Berridge was in London about this time and he wrote to Lady Huntingdon with the exciting news. Although there had been disagreements between the countess and Rowland, she wrote back to Berridge a gracious and supportive reply, and even hinted at a possible reconciliation.

I, who have known Mr Hill from his first setting out, can testify that no man ever engaged with more heartfelt earnestness in bringing captives from the strongholds of Satan into the glorious liberty of the gospel of our Immanuel; and it will require all the energies of his zealous and enterprising spirit to erect the standard of the cross in that part of London where ignorance and depravity prevail to such an awful degree.

Though I have seen sufficient cause to exclude him from serving in my chapels, *for the present*, yet I cordially rejoice in the success that has attended his faithful labours. I knew him when a youth at the university—when persecuted by his family—when in pecuniary distress—and he was as a son to me, received into my house, and preached for me everywhere. My heart's desire and prayer to God is, that this undertaking may prosper most abundantly, and that very many souls may there be gathered to the true Shiloh, such as will be his joy and crown in the day of the Lord Jesus Christ.

Lady Huntingdon was one of the first to help Rowland with a generous subscription. Many others liberally subscribed to the work, including Lord George Gordon, who gave £50. The managers of Whitefield's chapels also sanctioned the work and expressed their earnest desire to remain on friendly terms and to help in whatever way they could. The original estimate for the building of the chapel was £3000, but the actual cost exceeded £5000.

Surrey Chapel was nearly finished in the summer of 1783 and so opened for public worship on 8 June, a couple of months behind schedule. In many ways, the exterior resembled Lady Huntingdon's Spa Field's Chapel.

Outside Surrey Chapel

Apparently, Rowland once said that he preferred circular buildings 'because the devil could not occupy any one of the corners'. Whether this comment is true or not, round buildings were known to be better acoustically. The walls were made of brick and sixteen large windows on every side lighted the galleries, while smaller windows in the cupola lighted the body of the chapel. It had a high pulpit, which enabled the congregation to see and hear the preacher with ease. It seated 2500, although on special occasions 3000 people squeezed in, with many standing closely packed together in the aisles.

Many wonderful and extraordinary events occurred in and about the chapel, and many striking conversions; so much so, that when a distinguished minister preached one of the closing sermons at the chapel, the old building being about to be turned into a commercial warehouse, he

Inside Surrey Chapel

said, 'I believe there have been more souls saved in this chapel than there are bricks in these walls.'

On one occasion, as Rowland was returning from his customary walk to Blackfriars Bridge before the evening sermon, he heard a young man say to his friend, 'Let's go to old Rowland Hill's chapel and have some fun.' Rowland followed them into the chapel and gave orders to his doorkeeper to place them in the front seat of the gallery, right in front of the pulpit, and to fill up the seats around them so they could not leave. After the prayers Rowland gave out his text, 'The wicked shall be turned into hell, and all the nations that forget God' (Psalm 9:17), and immediately he looked full in the face of the two men, exclaiming, 'And there will be fun for you there!' The congregation, who knew all about Rowland's eccentricities, were sure he had a special reason for making such a remark; and when he repeated the comment each time he quoted his text, all looked in the same direction as Rowland to see who it was aimed at. Soon the two strangers became the centre of attention. One of the men was so struck by the sermon and Rowland's pointed comments that he fainted and had to be carried out by his friend. He returned to Surrey Chapel alone the following Sunday and was wonderfully converted. He later became a minister and before his death was chairman of the Congregational Union.

On an even more serious note, John Johnson assaulted his wife Jane on several occasions, and one of these occasions was on 8 June 1783 when she was returning from the opening of Surrey Chapel. John was standing at the door of their house when she returned. He asked her why she had taken the front door key and then struck her with his fist on the side of her face, knocking her down. She got up as soon as she was able and as she was going into the house, her husband took hold of her right hand thumb and bit it violently. It was so bruised that she lost the use of it and was soon under the care of an eminent and skilful surgeon.

Often those who came to the services out of curiosity or some other fancy were caught in the fisherman's net and became Rowland's loyal and close friends. Others, however, were determined to silence him. On one occasion, while Rowland was in the pulpit, he was shot at through one of the low windows next to Blackfriars Road. The bullet passed to the left of the pulpit and smashed through the window near the organ. The culprit was never caught, nor did he repeat the act; and whenever Rowland mentioned the incident he always gave thanks to God for his protection, for if the bullet had not risen in its projection, it passed so directly over him, that he almost certainly would have been hit.

After Rowland had settled at Surrey Chapel, he generally lived in London from November until the end of May, when he went to his beautiful home at Wotton-under-Edge, or started his itinerating work. Thus he described himself as 'the rector of Surrey Chapel, vicar of Wotton-under-Edge, and curate of all the fields and lanes throughout England and Wales'.

10. Rowland's generous heart

Immediately after Surrey Chapel was built Rowland, in accordance with his own generous mind and by example, set about training his own people to give liberally to many benevolent causes, to great effect. Twice when collections were made throughout the kingdom, in all churches and chapels, for the Patriotic Fund at Lloyd's and the subscription for the relief of the people of Germany, who had suffered the ravages of the French, the collections at Surrey Chapel were the largest raised at any one place. In alluding to these facts, Rowland, while preaching elsewhere for the benefit of the distressed, concluded his sermon with the words, 'Put your hands into your pockets, and be sure there is something in them when they come out. Let us have a good round, Surrey Chapel collection!'

On another occasion, in his desire to raise money, he probably raised a few eyebrows when he said, 'Let those who have bank notes (and I myself will be standing at the door) go out first; let those who have gold follow; let those who have silver go next; and let those who have copper only, stay till everybody else has gone out.' Similarly, he closed an address by saying, 'We are now about to have a collection; but before the plates are held at the doors we will sing a hymn, during which those who don't intend to

Rowland Hill (middle aged)

give may sneak off.' Another anecdote relates how before the collection was taken he ordered all the doors of the chapel to be locked except one, where he himself would stand and hold out the plate, that he might see how many of the congregation passed him without giving to the charity.

One of his members was on the committee of an auxiliary Tract Society, which had made several unsuccessful attempts to extend its operations. At last, it was decided to invite Rowland to take the chair of a public meeting at Mr Upton's chapel.

As our principal aim was to make the society known [said the member of Surrey Chapel], and to increase the number of quarterly purchasers of tracts, it was announced that there would be no collection... The chapel was crowded... The speakers, ever and anon, making facetious remarks upon the novelty and 'privilege' of attending a meeting at which there was to be no appeal for money. But, when the president arose to make his concluding remarks, he quite upset all our arrangements. 'What is this I hear,' said he, assuming an inimitable countenance, in which was blended a frown of pretended displeasure, with a half smile of playful humour, 'that there is to be no collection? So, then, you are going to disappoint these good people and send them away without affording them the opportunity of showing their zeal for the cause of God and their love for precious souls! I say,' he continued, throwing down two sovereigns upon the table, 'that there shall be a collection, and if no one else will contribute to it, I will.' The effect was most amusing. There was a general movement among the crowded assembly, and the cry of 'Plates, plates,' resounded from every part of the chapel. But, unfortunately, the plates were locked up—such a turn to our proceedings not being contemplated—and the key was not on the premises. No time could be lost, so I ran across the road to a chandler's shop and borrowed half-a-dozen dinner plates, which admirably answered our purpose. In the end a larger amount was obtained than ever we had collected before.

Some of these methods might be frowned upon today, but they demonstrate his eagerness to collect money for the poor and needy. W. Richards, in his funeral sermon for Rowland, remarked, 'He had a heart to feel for the miseries of his fellow creatures, and his hand was never slack in ministering to their necessities.'

Sometimes Rowland was caught out by his own generosity. He once became surety for a member of his church. The man failed and the pastor had to pay £1000, the amount of the bond. On the very same day of his 'liberality', he visited a friend, who noticed that he seemed unusually depressed. 'Why, Mr Hill, what's the matter with you today? You seem altogether heavy and uncomfortable.' Rowland, with tongue in cheek, replied, 'Heavy, sir, you are quite mistaken there, for I am a thousand pounds lighter than I was yesterday.'

One institution that started on 1 January 1784 at Surrey Chapel was a benevolent society for the relief and personal visitation of the sick and afflicted poor. Rowland laid down the rule that no one was to be excluded on account of their sect or party. Catholics and Protestants were to be treated equally.

On the evening of New Year's Day an anniversary service was held for the society. A sermon was preached and the most striking cases of need were read from the pulpit, accompanied by powerful comments and appeals from Rowland. Often the collection on these occasions amounted to more than £100. During one of these anniversary services a small parcel was handed to Rowland, who was then standing near the communion table. He unwrapped it to find a small pill-box, with the label, 'Rowland Hill's Benevolent Pills'. Inside, the box was full of gold coins. Without a moment's hesitation, Rowland looked round the congregation, in the midst of a fog that had filled the chapel, and remarked, 'I will take as many of these pills as you like to send me.' He then proceeded with the service.

Up to 1 January 1835, about twenty one months after Rowland's death, some 40,466 families, containing perhaps more than 200,000 people, had been visited, and over £23,000 spent on helping the needy. Amazingly, during the fifty years of the society's existence, not one of its visitors died from raging fever or from the other infectious diseases that were so prevalent in the families they visited.

At one time there were attached to Surrey Chapel no less than thirteen Sunday schools, containing some 3000 children, with an annual income, including collections, of nearly £250. Altogether over 60,000 children were instructed in the Christian faith and from these schools several ministers and missionaries were called to preach the everlasting gospel to the heathen world. On one Sunday, the clerk of Surrey Chapel announced the ordination service of a young man, who was about to go to a foreign land. He had been educated in the Surrey Chapel school. Interestingly, the minister supplying the pulpit had also been trained in the school and in the same class!

Rowland was fond of asking, 'Have you read Ellis's book on the South Sea Islands? Oh, worthy, sensible, good creature.' He then added quickly, 'He was a teacher in our Sunday school; he is an honour to us.'

One incident connected to the Sunday schools, Rowland often mentioned:

I remember that a poor man once met me at the corner of the street, and produced before me a little bit of paper, asking, 'Will you be so good as [to] read this for me?'

Says I to him, 'Can't you read yourself?'

'No, Sir; I was not born in the days in which there were many Sunday Schools; but my children can read very prettily, and they read to us after I have done my labour; and we never were so happy as since we have taken to read religious books, to look into our Bibles, and to pray that we may be governed by their contents.'

At Wotton too there was a Sunday school, which became a source of blessing to the neighbourhood.

Another interesting ministry that was joined to Surrey Chapel was a school of industry in the borough that clothed and educated twenty four girls. The school's wings contained alms houses for another twenty four poor women, who were given a comfortable room, sufficient fuel and four shillings a week towards their support. The only qualifications for entry were distress and a Christian character. The person applying must have been for at least seven years a regular attendant on the sacrament at a place of worship, not necessarily Surrey Chapel, and was required to bring testimonials of her moral and religious conduct from the minister. Rowland was very careful in selecting the right women and quick at detecting a hypocritical profession of faith.

An amusing incident occurred at one of the church meetings when an elderly woman approached Rowland curtseying and wanting to qualify herself for admission to an alms-house by becoming a member of the church.

'So you wish to join the Church?'

'If you please, sir.'

'Where have you been accustomed to hear the gospel?'

'At your *blessed* chapel, sir.'

'Oh! Indeed, at my *blessed* chapel; dear me! And how long have you attended with us?'

'For several years.'

'Do you think you have got any good by attending the chapel?'

'Oh, yes, sir! I have had many *blessed* seasons.'

'Indeed! Under whose ministry do you think you were led to feel yourself to be a sinner?'

'Under your *blessed* ministry.'

'Indeed! And do you think your heart is pretty good?'

'Oh, no, sir; it is a very bad one.'

'What! And do you come here with your bad heart and wish to join the Church?'

'Oh, sir! I mean that my heart is not worse than others; it is pretty good on the whole!'

'Indeed! That's more than I can say; I'm sure mine's bad enough. Well, have you heard that we are going to build some *blessed* alms-houses?'

'Yes, sir, I have.'

'Should you like to have one of them?'

Dropping a very low curtsey, she replied, 'Yes, sir, if you please.'

'I thought so. You may go about your business, my friend; you won't do for us.'

The members of his religious community formed a Dorcas society for the relief of poor married women, and a clothing society for supplying the needy with clothes at greatly reduced prices.

In reference to Surrey Chapel and all the various benevolent societies and charitable work that took place, it was said that:

No other place of worship in the kingdom, perhaps in the world, has ever, during the same space of time, been the seat of so much genuine piety and charity. Its ... contributions to all forms of charity have been more abundant, than those of any other sanctuary within or without the pale of the established church. It has set the example and taken the lead in all the most important schemes of Christian benevolence, by which the last forty-five years have been distinguished, and never was any former age so truly distinguished by such glory and virtue.

11. Extraordinary conversions

Rowland's own preaching was as powerful as ever at this time in London and elsewhere. John Griffin heard him in 1792 for 'a part of four Sabbaths', when he was 'strongly excited' over some recent publications by Joseph Priestley. Griffin said that 'he seemed to throw the whole force of his mind into a course of arguments in defence of the divinity and atonement of Christ, which I then felt to be lucid, cogent, and conclusive'. He went on to describe his preaching:

His appeals to the conscience were irresistible, like a sharp two-edged sword; many stout-hearted sinners were wounded to the quick... His appeals pierced the hearts even of those whose consciences were seared as with a hot iron.

His ministry was powerfully persuasive... When his spirit was under the unction of the Spirit of God, and his mind in a good frame for preaching, he poured forth the affections of his heart in persuasive strains of expostulations and reasoning with the sinner, till vast multitudes were melted into tears of godly sorrow for sin, while others were excited to the most lively affection to Christ, and to spiritual joys arising from the hope that God was reconciled unto them, and felt the internal evidence of their reconciliation.

Regardless of the opinion of others, Rowland often thought little of his own ministry. 'I have just finished the labours of the day,' he wrote. 'How poorly done, though done with all our might!... Oh, for hearts full of Christ's love, and lives devoted to his glory! But what a mere slug do I find myself in the divine life! Quicken me, O Lord, according to thy word.'

His preaching, however, resulted in the extraordinary conversions of several notorious infidels and persecutors, who afterwards became staunch supporters of what they once tried to destroy. One man, a member of an infidel club, came to Surrey Chapel one Sunday evening out of curiosity and returned home crying for mercy and pardon. A few days later he went to see Rowland to ask him what he must do to be saved, and the burden of guilt was removed. He worked in a time consuming business, but spent his free time in the service of the God he had once despised.

A second man was a 'drunkard, swearer and cruel persecutor of his wife, who belonged to Mr Wesley's Society'. One evening, after he had been to chapel, he received his wife so kindly that she was astonished. He said, 'I have been to hear Mr Hill;—I am a sinner; you were right, I was wrong—I hope I shall never be unkind to you again, but that we shall walk together in the same way.' There were many similar instances, and scores were aroused out of their carelessness and indifference by the powerful teaching of God's word.

Some people were drawn to Surrey Chapel by a report of Rowland's odd sayings in the pulpit; but instead of observations that made them smile or laugh, they heard 'an awakening appeal to sinners, that sent them as trembling and weeping penitents to the throne of grace'. One young man, who went to the chapel to have 'a little fun', was soundly converted and afterwards became a regular supply for Rowland. Many of the anecdotes told about his eccentricities are untrue, although sometimes he did introduce into his sermons illustrations that he acknowledged afterwards would have been better left out; 'but,' he would add, 'the queer thought came into my head, and out it came, and I could not help it; I wish it had kept in though'. Almost always he felt low in his spirits after he had given into temptation in this way, and regretted using levity while engaged in the solemn service of the pulpit.

Once a friend heard him preach a sermon in Brighton, in which there were many humorous remarks and a considerable degree of laughter in the congregation. 'This was followed by such an awful address to their consciences, and a pathos so deep and melting, that there was scarcely an individual present who did not weep.' In the evening the conversation in the house where Rowland was staying was 'light and lively'. Soon after Rowland had left the room to go to bed, his friend thought he heard someone in the passage, and so went to look. There was Rowland at the foot of the stairs.

He feared he was unwell; but on enquiring the reason of his remaining there, he discovered him to be in deep agony of mind, to which he gave vent in confessions of sorrow at having been such a trifler, and mourned over his unseasonable drollery with the simplicity of a child. Before he went to his room, he said, 'I never wish to say a single word to excite a smile, which would prevent an immediate approach to God in all the solemnity of spiritual prayer.'

This scene was most affecting and demonstrates how deeply he mourned over succumbing to the natural sprightliness of his mind when, in his view, such behaviour clouded his real usefulness, and denigrated the character of a preacher of the gospel.

During the French revolution, Rowland chose to steer clear of politics and to preach the gospel of Christ as the surest antidote to disloyalty and error. Many were curious to hear him at this time who were dissatisfied with the role of the government and who were eager to challenge the order in society. Some who sat under his ministry were so impressed by his sermons, that they experienced a complete change of heart by God's grace, which led to new 'heavenly principles and conduct'. Rowland commented that the state 'receives daily benefit by the gospel we attempt to disseminate, as we have the fullest evidence that such as were enemies to the Bible, and enemies to the government, are now the friends of both, and that from the best and firmest principles; and even such as are suspected of disloyalty to the constitution are refused connection with us'.

Rowland recorded some of the powerful effects of the gospel. He mentioned two brothers in business and members of a 'revolution society', who out of curiosity attended Surrey Chapel one day.

It pleased God to impress the word home upon their hearts, and from mere monsters they became men and Christians indeed. The joy introduced into their families was inexpressible, and the credit brought to religion very considerable. When they came to me to be admitted to the Lord's table, they freely told me, though with much compunction, what they originally were... Upon their conversion to God, all their former connections were immediately renounced, and strict adherence to public and private worship was seriously attended to, and a large number of their apprentices, led on by them in the same way, were wonderfully recovered from the like snare.

From these two men Rowland learned that the first objective of the rebels was to seduce their followers into the principles of infidelity through Paine's *Age of Reason*. When that has been accomplished, the leaders could speak with confidence about their 'work' and their plans would become 'the most daring and dangerous'.

One of Paine's disciples and a member of a corresponding society was drawn to the chapel by its fine organ. As he listened to the sermon, the word of God entered his heart and he was converted. He became a devoted Christian, the secretary of a leading society connected with the chapel, and an enthusiastic supporter of Rowland. His former friends, having missed him at their club, asked after him. 'My views of reform,' replied the good man, 'have undergone a change—I once thought it my duty to try and reform others; now, I think that the best plan is to begin reformation at *home*—and when that work is effectually done, then to try and reform my neighbours.'

In the autumn of 1793 Rowland visited Ireland and pulpits were open to him in Dublin and other places. In Dublin his 'presence and advice were peculiarly useful to those ministers of the Church of England who were at that time suffering much obloquy and persecution for the faithful testimony which they bore to the great doctrines of the Reformation'. From Dublin he wrote to his friend William Bull, who read the letter in the Surrey Chapel pulpit. 'The contents were to the effect that many students in the university and many of the fellows are awakened. They preach Christ. The churches are opened to them; and they go in crowds to hear Mr Hill, and have him to visit them in the college daily. All their time is taken up by the Bible and prayer. This is glorious news.' The warm-hearted Irish heard Rowland with deep attention and he was held in high veneration particularly in Dublin. He returned home having greatly enjoyed his visit. In the same year when a powerful appeal was made for the distressed weavers in Spitalfields, Rowland was forthright in speaking out for their support, and at Surrey Chapel he raised £220. 17s. 6d., which was by far the largest collection made.

In 1796 Rowland made another visit to Ireland. Letters from his Irish hearers testify to the work of God that occurred among them while he was there. During his return from this second tour he was mercifully preserved from shipwreck, to which he often referred with much thankfulness. The captain of the ship was a habitual swearer, and so Rowland challenged him by saying, 'Captain, let us have fair play. You must not have all the swearing yourself. It's my turn next. You must not swear again till I have quite done.' These comments had the desired effect, and no more swearing was heard from the captain for the rest of the voyage.

On his return from Ireland, Rowland prepared to tour Scotland, where many were ready to receive him with great enthusiasm. The people of the north were about to discover, not only the power of his preaching, but the warmth of his character.

12. Touring Scotland

In 1798 Rowland made his first visit to Scotland. He was then in the meridian of life; and, as one has described him, a somewhat

…handsome man, of a tall commanding stature, with highly expressive features, a keen searching eye, and a singularly fine nose, which was bold and aquiline, but in exact proportion to his face. His voice, too, was very powerful; and, at times, melodious. When he first entered the pulpit, his nervous agitation was often extreme, and every member of his body seemed to shake. He gave out his text indistinctly, and almost inaudibly; and it was only as he proceeded that his tones rose, and he became colloquial or humorous. He had the art of instantly arresting the attention of his hearers! and as he seemed to address them from the fervour of his own feelings, he often produced a strong effect on theirs. His action, too, though often ludicrously distorted, would sometimes, when he leaned forward on the sconces of the pulpit, become truly graceful and dignified.

At the end of the eighteenth century it was the custom for popular English preachers to spend a few weeks of the year visiting Scotland, or the destitute parts of their own country. They travelled, not as charity workers, but as evangelists, to stir up the people to the concerns of the gospel and in this way many sinners were led to Christ. Rowland was invited by a group of zealous Christians, who had leased the Circus in Edinburgh as a chapel. The Circus, at the head of Leith Walk, had for some time been used by a congregation belonging to the Relief Secession while their own chapel was being rebuilt, but they had since left it. As it was a large place of worship, it was decided to ask Rowland to come and open it and preach there for the first few Sundays, and to remain in Scotland for five or six weeks, preaching to the people wherever and whenever he could. He agreed.

The services were held at seven o'clock in the morning and six in the evening so they would not interfere with other churches. Robert Haldane in his account of the opening of the Circus found in his *Address*, comments, 'The multitudes that heard him, and the spirit of attention that seemed to be excited, encouraged us to go on.' When the Circus Church was constituted in January 1799, no less than 310 persons wanted to unite in its communion, many of whom had been converted by Rowland's preaching in and around Edinburgh.

His first evening in Scotland (Thursday 26 July) was spent at Langholm, in the county of Dumfries, where an annual public fair happened to be taking place. In his journal he described it as 'a downright revel; dancing, drunkenness and lasciviousness seemed to be the principal motive which had brought them together. In England I scarce ever saw a more disgraceful assemblage.' In order to rest his horse, it was necessary for him to spend the night 'in this temporary hell'. To avoid the 'wretched tumult' he took an evening's walk out of the town, by the River Esk, where he met the minister of the parish, who, 'with much hospitality', offered him every accommodation his house could afford from the confusion of the town, but he declined it as he had already secured a private lodging. While talking by the river, James Haldane and John Aikman, passed by, both itinerating in that area and hoping to do good to the crowds that assembled at the fair. It appears they did not join the conversation.

These gentlemen were then unknown to me [Rowland wrote in his journal]. I was told [presumably by the minister of the parish], but in very candid language, their errand and design; that it was a marvellous circumstance, quite a phenomenon, that an East India captain, a gentleman of good family and connexions, should turn out an itinerant preacher; that he should travel from town to town, and all against his own interest and character... This information was enough for me. I immediately sought out the itinerants diligently, and found them in the same tumultuous mess, and at the

James Haldane

same inn. When I inquired for them of the landlady [of the inn], she told me she supposed I meant the two priests that were in her house; but she could not satisfy me what religion they were of. The two priests, however, and myself soon met; and to our mutual satisfaction passed the evening together.

The following morning Rowland headed for Edinburgh, while his two new friends stayed to complete their preaching tour. At Hawick, Rowland saw for the first time a Scottish funeral, which was conducted without prayer or a minister. On mentioning to a bystander that their funerals were soon over, an old woman piped up and told him prayers were no use to the dead. To this he agreed, but 'suggested that the people of Scotland lost an excellent opportunity of doing good to the living, if they could do nothing for the dead'.

He reached Edinburgh on Saturday 28 July and was received with great kindness and affection 'at the hospitable abode of Mr James Haldane, in George Street'. The following day, he opened the Circus, 'supposed to contain above 2500 people'.

Rowland stayed in Edinburgh for the week, preaching on Tuesday at Robinson's Chapel of Ease. On Thursday 2 August he preached in a timber yard at Leith to two thousand people, saying, 'Plain language is the only profitable language for sinners like these.' The following day four thousand persons heard him on the Calton Hill.

The next Lord's Day he preached three times: at seven in the morning and again at noon, both in the Circus; but in the evening the crowds attending his preaching were so large that the Circus could not contain half the numbers who wanted to hear him, and there was a scare that the galleries were giving way under the weight of the people. So he moved to the Calton Hill, a natural amphitheatre, where he preached from a platform to a gathering numbering at least 10,000. He illustrated and enforced the love of God to man from the *Parable of the Prodigal Son*. After the service the crowd silently dispersed, many for the first time concerned about their souls and eternity. Some old women, watching the solemn procession file past their front doors, called out to a party of soldiers, 'Eh, sirs, what will become of us now! What will this turn to! The very sodgers are ganging to hear preaching.'

Rowland's method of preaching, especially his quaint interjections and anecdotes, was a 'complete novelty in Scotland', but that did not lessen its effect. Once, when preaching to a congregation composed mainly of weavers, he abruptly exclaimed, 'O ye weavers, doesn't the shuttle go sweet when the love of God is burning in your hearts?' John Campbell, the well-known missionary to Africa, noted:

His addresses were novel to us all, and the burst of zeal he manifested for the salvation of his hearers was equally novel; the intermingling of striking facts relating to himself and others was what we were not accustomed to. No man could preach better Gospel sermons than those we had been favoured with, but his manner of telling the truth was so different that we seemed as if we had got into a new world. Had he come immediately after the days of George Whitefield, he would not have been so great a novelty; but the generation who heard that man of God had passed away, and a new one had arisen in their room.

During some of his sermons the eternal world appeared to be next door to us, and but a step between us and the judgement day, which seemed to cause a shaking among our dry bones.

Rowland's preaching and manner produced a singular impression on the minds of the people.

On entering the pulpit, he knelt to pray [it was reported].

'He's a Roman Catholic,' said one.

He concluded his public supplications with the Lord's Prayer.

'Oh, I ken he's of the English kirk,' said another.

When Rowland began to preach, he said, 'I understand you are fond of lectures in Scotland, and so I shall adopt your favourite plan.' He soon told rather an amusing anecdote, and at the end of it exclaimed, 'But I've forgotten my lecture,' which produced a general impression that the poor gentleman was a little cracked. These feelings, however, soon passed away, and his lively and animated style, and his pungent and eloquent appeals to the conscience, led many to cry, 'What shall we do to be saved?' A respectable Scotch minister ... stated that he never heard an anecdote from a pulpit, in his native land, until Mr Hill began his itinerant labours there.

Rowland was not surprised by the interest his preaching aroused, for he had learned to expect great things. 'While we are straitened in our expectations,' he said, 'the blessing is withheld; but when our hearts are enlarged, the more we ask, the more we have.'

It was probably at about this time in Scotland that Rowland was introduced to an aged minister, who was very much like Rowland in godliness and eccentricity. For some time the old man closely studied Rowland and then at last said, 'Weel, I have been looking for some teem at the leens of your face.' 'And what do you think of it?' replied Rowland. 'Why, I am thinking that if the grace of God hadna changed your heart, you would ha been a most tremendous rogue.' Rowland laughed heartily and said, 'Well, you have just hit the nail on the head.'

On Monday 6 August, Rowland, accompanied by Robert Haldane, visited Stirling and Dumblane, 'where he saw the seat of action of that best of men, Archbishop Leighton, who was everything that was wise, just and good'. He then went to Crieff, Dunkeld, Perth and Kinross, and his preaching was accompanied by the same excitement as in Edinburgh.

He returned to Edinburgh on Sunday 12 August and preached in the morning and evening at the Circus. The following day he moved on to Glasgow, where he spoke in the evening in the churchyard of the old cathedral. The scene was 'most solemn'. Underneath us,' he added, 'were the remains, I may venture to say, of millions waiting for the resurrection. Here I stood on a widely extended space, covered, or nearly covered, with the living, all immortals—five thousand, I should suppose, at least. What solemn work to address such multitudes! *Who is sufficient for these things?*' He preached from Isaiah 60:19 and exclaimed, 'Could we but explain to sinners, and make them feel that God, a God in Christ, is their glory, and that it is their privilege to glorify God in return, we should have more than abundant recompense for all our little toil in a work so glorious and great.'

Although he was very tired from his exertions, he agreed to preach the following morning at eight o'clock at Paisley, and preached to another huge assembly in the yard of the church over which Witherspoon had once presided. He remarked,

I passed the evening at the house of the truly affectionate son of that truly apostolic man, the late Dr Gillies, the author of the *Memoirs of Mr Whitefield's Life*. His house was filled with good ministers of different denominations, all living in affectionate love and cordiality with each other. This makes Paisley the paradise of Scotland. Indeed, hell would be a paradise if love were there; and an earthly paradise is little better than hell, if love be absent. My soul loves Paisley, for there I believe Christians love each other.

Rowland's third stop in Edinburgh was on Saturday 18 August. On Sunday even larger crowds gathered to listen to him. He preached at seven in the morning and again at eleven, when the Circus was full. 'It was now,' he said, 'quite out of the question to preach within doors on the Lord's Day evenings,' so later that day he preached on the Calton Hill, where he addressed the most solemn congregation he had seen for many years. He estimated there were at least 15,000, although some supposed a larger crowd, who heard him preach in a way calculated to alarm sinners, 'from the consideration of the immortality of the soul, and the awfulness of eternity'.

During this third week Rowland continued to visit other parts of the country and was accompanied by James Haldane, who took the place of his elder brother. On Tuesday evening they reached Dundee, where Rowland preached to 2000 people out of doors, and again the following morning in the same place. They travelled on to St Andrews, where they experienced 'some indications of opposition', which led Rowland to think that after being treated in the west like a gentleman, he was about to be treated as an apostle, with persecution; though he admitted, after such indulgences, he owned no great appetite for such sour sauce! He preached at eight in the morning, with less interruption than he had anticipated, and again in the evening.

On his way back to Edinburgh, on the Thursday evening and Friday morning, Rowland preached at Kirkcaldy, where he was severely rebuked by an old man, one of the elders of the church, for omitting the second psalm. His apology was that he had to cross the water and did not have time for another psalm. He thought two psalms no more necessary than two sermons, and that such things were optional, as time and opportunity allowed. He crossed the water to Leith and preached in the evening to 2000 people in Mr Shirreiff's park.

On Sunday 26 August he preached at seven in the morning in the Circus, which was quite crowded, and in the evening on the Calton Hill to between 15,000 and 20,000 people. He was engaged to preach at Musselburgh, but was not well enough, so James Haldane took his place. He quickly recovered and the following day preached at Dalkeith, and at Musselburgh on the Thursday evening. On Friday he preached his last sermon at Leith, where 3000 people heard him. Sunday 2 September was his last Sabbath in Edinburgh and he preached three times. The Circus could hardly contain the numbers who attended the early and noon sermons.

In the evening he preached his 'last sermon, save one, in this vicinity, on the Calton Hill. Although there was a threat of rain, the congregation was 'astonishingly large' (about 18,000 to 20,000 people). A public collection was taken up for the use of the charity workhouse, which the magistrates of the city gratefully received. It appears that the collection came to about £30, almost entirely composed of halfpence and penny pieces, and the entire sum was taken away in a wheelbarrow.

The following day he again preached three times: in the morning he addressed the children in Lady Maxwell's School, afterwards the unfortunate women at the Philanthropic Asylum, and in the evening, for the last time, at the Circus. He then set out for England, accompanied by Robert Haldane. The journey took nearly three weeks. They travelled to Dunbar, where an unusual incident took place, which has often been exaggerated in order to highlight Rowland's eccentricities. The story, as told by Robert Haldane, with his usual accuracy, occurred on the Wednesday morning. They were just about to set off in Rowland's carriage when his horse was found to be lame. A farrier was called, who, after examination, said that the main problem was in the horse's shoulder, that the disease was incurable, and that they might shoot the poor animal as soon as they pleased. Rowland, however, was not prepared to follow such advice. He stayed at Cunningham's house for two more days.

In the evening Mr Hill conducted family worship, and after the supplications for the family, domestics and friends, added a fervent prayer for the restoration of the valuable animal, which had carried him so many thousands of miles, preaching the everlasting Gospel to his fellow-sinners. Mr Cunningham, who was remarkable for the staid and orderly, if not stiff, demeanour … was not only surprised but grieved, and even scandalized at what he deemed so great an impropriety. He remonstrated with his guest. But Mr Hill stoutly defended his conduct by an appeal to Scripture, and the superintending watchfulness of Him without whom a sparrow falls not to the ground. He persisted in his prayer during the two days he continued at Dunbar, and although he left the horse in a hopeless state, to follow in charge of his servant, by easy stages, he continued his prayer night and morning, till one day at an inn in Yorkshire, while the two travellers were sitting at breakfast, they heard a horse and chaise trot briskly into the yard, and looking out, saw that Mr Hill's servant had arrived, bringing up the horse perfectly restored. Mr Hill did not fail to return thanks, and begged his fellow-traveller to consider, whether the minuteness of his prayers had deserved the censure which had been directed against them.

Rowland's horse carried its master on many more journeys after its illness.

On the Sunday before he arrived home he preached in the evening at Rotherham to 10,000 people in the open air from Acts 3:19. At first the bells of a neighbouring church interrupted his sermon, but as soon as the ringers were told he was preaching, they kindly stopped and he was able to continue in peace. Just as the service was about to conclude a man, waving a drawn sword, tried to force his way through the congregation to where Rowland was standing. 'While he brandished his sword with great vehemence, and struggled hard to reach me,' said Rowland, 'the people arrested him, threw him down, and disarmed him. Through the kind providence of God no one was in the least hurt, nor was the tranquillity of our meeting so much disturbed as might have been expected from such an extraordinary event. Upon the seizure of this unhappy man he appeared to be entirely insane.'

He reached Wotton on Saturday 22 September and found all to be well, which caused him to cry, 'Indulgent God, thy name be praised.'

During this first tour of Scotland, it was believed that at least 200 were converted through his preaching, some of whom 'notorious for their vice and profligacy'. One friend, who heard many of the sermons, frequently remarked, 'Whenever I listened to him, eternity appeared to be next door to me.'

Rowland returned to Scotland the following year, but regrettably a fierce controversy with the General Assembly marred the pleasure and usefulness of this second tour and there is little in his journal that is profitable to recall.

13. Vaccination against smallpox

At the beginning of the nineteenth century, Rowland became deeply interested in a vaccination against smallpox, a disease that was desolating many towns and hamlets in the land. Dr Edward Jenner, who lived at Berkeley, Gloucestershire, after many successful experiments, discovered what was then believed by some to be an absolute preventive of the disease. Rowland calmly investigated the subject and on many occasions spoke with Dr Jenner, who lived in the vicinity of Wotton. He became convinced that it was his duty to advocate and practise a general vaccination, saying, 'This is the very thing for me.' After preaching he would often announce, 'I am ready to vaccinate tomorrow morning as many children as you choose; and if you wish them to escape that horrid disease, the smallpox, you will bring them.' Rowland's opinion was against the prevailing view of the medical profession. In fact, many violently opposed the practice of vaccination and some doctors strove to prejudice the public against it.

William Jay was once with Rowland when someone started to speak disrespectfully of vaccination, saying there was something 'very disagreeable and offensive in communicating a disease from a filthy beast into a human being'. Rowland immediately responded by exclaiming, 'A filthy beast, sir! Why, a cow is one of the most agreeable of all animals; everything about her is

Dr Edward Jenner

wholesome and useful; we get odour from her breath; she supplies our tables with meat and butter and cream and cheese; and I assure you, sir, I would rather eat a cow than a Christian.'

The opposition caused Rowland in March 1806 to publish a small pamphlet (72 pages) called *Cowpock Inoculation Vindicated and Recommended, from Matters of Fact*, which he dedicated to the Duke of Bedford, then Lord Lieutenant of Ireland. It had an extensive circulation and removed the prejudices of many against a vital discovery.

According to the pamphlet, Rowland's first efforts to spread the blessings of vaccination were early in the summer of 1804 in and about Wotton, where nearly 1200 people were vaccinated. It was so successful that the disease, which had been rampant, disappeared from that place. At Portsmouth, where he exchanged pulpits with his friend Edward Griffin, whom he instructed 'in the art of vaccination', he vaccinated many, but the vaccine failed because it had been exposed to too much light and air. During the autumn, while on a visit to Bristol, he successfully vaccinated hundreds. When he returned to London, he inoculated 80 people from Clapham and put a stop to the ravages of the disease there.

The following year (1805) at Chatham, where smallpox was particularly prevalent, having urged the people to meet him at three different places of worship, he inoculated 320 people in two days. He moved on to Frome, where his friend John Sibree wanted to introduce vaccination. At Shepton Mallet, he encountered the hostility of the people towards vaccination, in spite of the fact that seventy persons had recently died from smallpox. He recommended vaccination in his sermon on the Lord's Day, and about 200 people responded the following morning. He also instructed Priestley, the minister of Shepton Mallet, on how to inoculate others.

During a summer's excursion to South Wales, with the help of others, he inoculated about 1100 people in Pembrokeshire. 'Thus,' he said, 'the poor people, in and about the neighbourhood of Haverfordwest … are mercifully secured from a contagious disease, which would very probably have soon made its inroads among them: while no less than three hundred in the town of Carmarthen, at a distance of about 30 miles from Haverfordwest, were carried to the grave the victims of that awful plague.' On 11 March 1806, he received a letter from W. G. Meylett of Haverfordwest, who said, 'There has been no one in the country who has had the smallpox after vaccination; nor have I observed any other disagreeable symptoms follow the complaint, except for two who soon recovered.'

After detailing the opposition to the plan, Rowland stated,

I have next solemnly to assert, that having inoculated in different places, not less than 4840 subjects; independent of 3720 and upwards, which have been inoculated at Surrey Chapel School Room; I have not as yet, met with ONE SINGLE FAILURE, though upon the repetitions of my visits, I have at all times made it a point to enquire, with the utmost diligence in my power; nor yet in any one point of view, have I seen any of those distressful consequences which have been brought forward with so much *art* and *downright falsehood*, to alarm the fears and terrify the imaginations of the public.

Once a week he inoculated children who were brought to him from Wotton and the neighbourhood, and thanks to his support one of the most effective vaccine boards in London was established in Surrey Chapel. He was totally at ease vaccinating children, talking kindly to their parents while reassuring their frightened sons and daughters in a most good natured manner.

The benefits of this new discovery spread far and wide. Dr Lettsom, an eminent doctor of his day, informed Rowland that a doctor in Madras had inoculated 250,000 British subjects and Gentoos, and that the Brahmins called it the *dew of heaven*, because before vaccination usually nine out of ten lost their lives from the disease. The vaccine had been administered in camps and armies, arresting smallpox in its progress 'without the least inconvenience whatever'.

Rowland calculated the beneficial results of inoculating 10,000 persons and remarked,

We will take the average of deaths by the smallpox to be rather under one in six: the vaccination of ten thousand subjects, therefore, produces the preservation of *one thousand six hundred lives.*

After having said so much I need not add, that next to attending upon the functions of my own calling, I never undertook a work so satisfactory to my own mind... Let our exertions be universal, immediate and zealous, and I am very sure a death by the smallpox will be brought forward as a very rare instance indeed; in short, I believe that no one disease will be less fatal than that which is now so much the dreaded scourge of the human race.

Happily, Rowland lived long enough to see, to a large extent, the removal of the prejudice against the smallpox vaccination for which he had fought so nobly.

Rowland and Dr Jenner remained good friends, and although the doctor did not embrace Rowland's religious views and feelings, he had the highest regard for his character and frequently attended his ministry at Cheltenham. At times he was 'forcibly struck with the deep tone of the zealous preacher's piety and glowing anticipation of happiness, in a spiritual state of being'. Once Rowland introduced Dr Jenner to a nobleman by saying, 'Allow me to present to your lordship my friend Dr Jenner, who has been the means of saving more lives than any other man.' Dr Jenner bowed and replied with great earnestness, 'Ah! would I like you, could save souls.' Sidney remembered watching these two men play with an old eagle in Dr Jenner's garden at Berkeley, 'with all the sportive interest of boys'.

At this time of life, Rowland's ministry was made very useful to some Gloucestershire farmers, whose lives were radically transformed and who became shining examples of the power of the gospel. One individual, in his youth, attended 'every scene of rural dissipation within his reach'. He was a fighter, a horse racer, a midnight rioter at fairs and revels, until the grace of God changed his heart and life. He then became a zealous follower of Christ—a peacemaker, generous to the needy, industrious and hard working.

Rowland had a great regard for this farmer, who had a naturally fervent spirit. Sometimes when he looked at his aged minister, a tear rolled down his cheek as he remembered that he was the first messenger of peace to comfort his soul. He took great care of his employees and the Lord prospered him.

The *Evangelical Biography* relates a further incident of Rowland and a 'fighter'. The great preacher was engaged to preach in a town where violent opposition was expected and a famous boxer stood ready to attack him; so Rowland resorted to the following strategy:

Having ascended the pulpit, and satisfied himself from the appearance of the pugilist [boxer], that he was not inaccessible to flattery, he beckoned him to the pulpit stairs, and told him that he was come to preach to those people, in the hope of doing them good—that some opposition had been threatened—that he had been told of his strength and skill in self-defence, and had full confidence in his powers:—that he therefore should place himself in his hands, rely on his protection, and begged the favour of his company to ride with him in his carriage after the service to dinner! The man felt the full force of the compliment; all his animosity was removed; he declared his readiness to defend the preacher in case of any insult being offered, and was as good as his word. He accompanied Mr Hill to dinner, and ever after boasted of the honour which the latter had conferred upon him.

In the early months of 1808, Rowland turned his attention to Cheltenham and how he could introduce the gospel there. The parish church was not able to accommodate all the worshippers who came to the town, which was becoming quite a fashionable resort, so Rowland, with some good men in the neighbourhood, planned to build a chapel between High Street and St George's Place to attract the visitors. Through his influence and example, subscriptions were soon raised to erect a large place of worship. A gentleman who lived in the town also helped him.

The first stone was laid 5 July 1808 and Rowland preached on the occasion to a large congregation (about 3000), 'in an energetic and appropriate speech'. It was completed and opened for divine

William Jay

service on 2 August 1809. Rowland preached in the morning and William Jay in the evening to very crowded congregations.

Whenever Rowland visited Cheltenham the chapel was crowded and he continued to preach in it to huge congregations until the year of his death. 'From this pulpit,' remarked Sidney, 'he delivered some of his finest sermons; and his dignified appearance, energy of manner, and widely extended fame, attracted persons of every rank, not a few of whom greatly profited by the truths they heard.'

14. 'Light afflictions'

Rowland was surrounded by all sorts of people, partly because of his fame as a preacher, and partly because of his lively personality. With most of them he was reserved, except those who possessed his confidence. Many thought they knew him well because he was courteous, polite and cheerful with those he respected, and the readiness of his wit and humour caused him to talk in an apparently unrestrained manner; but few were truly acquainted with the 'movements of his mind or the events of his early days'. Some presumed on his kindness, which he bore patiently and with the hope of doing good. If in conversation he became suspicious of another's motives or actions, and these suspicions were confirmed, he could be harsh and abrupt with the offender and would not grant them a second interview.

Once an individual, who had brought great dishonour to the gospel, met him at his front door as he was leaving his house, and with a hypocritical greeting, cried, 'How do you do, Mr Hill; I am delighted to see you once more.' Rowland made no immediate answer, and then, with an air of amazement, exclaimed, 'What! Aren't you hanged yet?' and returned to the house until the unwelcome and astonished visitor had left.

Many people came to see him with all sorts of requests. Once the footman ushered in 'a most romantic looking lady', who walked towards Rowland in such a way that caused him to retreat towards the fireplace.

'Divine shepherd' [she began].

'Upon my word, ma'am!'

'I hear you have great influence with the royal family.'

'Well, ma'am, and did you hear anything else?'

'Now seriously, sir—my son has most wonderful poetic powers. Sir, his poetry is of a sublime order—noble, original, fine.'

'Well, I wonder what will come next,' muttered Mr Hill, in a low tone.

'Yes, sir, pardon the liberty, and therefore I called to ask you to get him made *Poet Laureate.*'

'Ma'am, you might as well ask me to get him made Archbishop of Canterbury!'

The mother of the poetic genius withdrew, looking highly indignant at the fit of laughter it was impossible to suppress.

Rowland was constantly interrupted as people came to his door and on most occasions he received the visitors kindly and with good humour and listened to their requests with sincerity, even when they were a little unusual.

In the autumn of 1811 Rowland was riding his favourite cream coloured horse, Bob, through a steep and rugged ravine, which was the shortest route to a village in a neighbouring valley, where he was going to preach. Suddenly the horse stumbled over one of the many large stones scattered on the path, and fell with his whole weight on Rowland. The animal lay quite still while his master pulled himself free. Rowland was badly bruised, with two broken ribs, and confined to bed for some weeks. During this time a severe inflammation settled in his right eye. He was not able to preach, so he stayed at Wotton till near Christmas, when his eye became so bad that he went to London to consult the celebrated Mr Ware. He travelled with Sidney and it took them two days. Rowland was 'mostly silent and dejected, complaining of great pain' until Sidney commented, 'There is Eton, sir.' He then seemed to forget his discomfort and spoke to Sidney in the kindest manner about his religious feelings when a schoolboy, along with 'beautiful remarks on the dedication of our youth to God, and the pleasure of the remembrance of having spent it in his service'. On arriving in London he went straight to see Mr Ware.

When he finally reached home, he rose into a 'frame of the most exalted piety, and walked up and down the room, breathing forth resignation to his chastening Father's will, with all the fervour of a sanctified use of affliction'. A minister who was present observed, 'I never saw him in a more holy state of mind.' Rowland, in referring to this affliction, remarked, 'God has laid me on one side, has incapacitated me for his work to humble me, to make me feel that I am nothing in his cause, and that I may more justly value the privilege of labouring for his glory.' Soon, however, due to the skill of Mr Ware, he was restored to his people, who welcomed him back with great affection.

A couple of years later, while on his way back from Wotton to London, Rowland was struck down by a severe and painful disease. His friends were deeply concerned and were anxious to get him to London as soon as possible to receive the necessary medical attention. He expressed his feelings in a letter to one of the members of Surrey Chapel.

My days must be nearly ended, and consequently my life is comparatively of little worth. Still may the languid efforts of my declining days prove not an unacceptable offering before him, by whose divine power our weakest efforts may be crowned with the most abundant success. At present, however, I am obliged to give way to disease, and though perhaps nothing dangerous, yet exceedingly painful and lowering to the constitution. Yesterday I suffered severely, and today am very feverish, weak and low, and how I shall be able to accomplish my journey to town, as yet I cannot tell.

He wanted to travel to London as soon as he was able, but even if he had been in town he would not have been able to perform the accustomed services of the chapel. He recognised that his suffering was 'from the hand of God' and that he had no reason to complain, 'having been possessed of so much health and strength, for so many years. I have,' he said, 'been favoured beyond most: God forbid that these light afflictions should excite the most distant murmurings, from one that has cause for the most abundant thankfulness before God.'

One problem that his doctors and friends had during his illness was to stop him preaching. Only total physical inability seemed to persuade him to desist. His wife said, 'The exertion of preaching is injurious to Mr Hill, but I find it difficult to keep him from it.' Eventually he was moved to London, where Dr Babington and Mr Cline attended him with such skill and kindness that he began to recover. The former called so often and was so attentive to his needs that Rowland was worried that his frequent visits would interfere with his own interests. The doctor replied, 'Mr Hill, I shall be happy indeed to be made in any way the instrument of your recovery, for I shall not only have the pleasure of seeing you in the enjoyment of health, but shall have conferred a benefit upon numbers, to whom your ministry is made useful.'

Rowland was a good patient, in spite of his restless temperament and impatience at being 'shut up'. On 5 December 1814 he replied to a letter from his friend O. P. Wathen, who had written to Mrs Hill inquiring about his health.

Yes, the Lord in infinite wisdom and goodness has chastened and afflicted me, but has not given me over to death. Only this day se'nnight I was in such a state, that if the Lord had not put a speedy termination to my disease, it must have speedily terminated my life; but, by the blessing of God on some of the best medical help that London affords, I am still preserved, and O that it may be for his future glory, as far as he condescends to engage me as an instrument in his hands for the future good of his church and people!

Rowland regarded his recovery as a 'short respite, rather than a long reprieve', although he was ready to work for as long as the Lord designed. He was still convalescing but gaining strength all the time, and he could hardly wait to be 'set at work'.

The first time he went for a walk after his illness, on a fine winter's day, it was with much persuasion that he put on his greatcoat. In the streets all sorts of people congratulated him: tradesmen, who ran out of their shops; passers by greeted him, and everyone he visited was delighted to see him up and about. When he returned his servant asked, 'Sir, where is your greatcoat?' 'That's more than I can tell you,' replied Rowland laughing, 'but I'll tell you where I have been, and you must go a hunting after it by and by.' Rowland often forgot where he put his clothes and Sidney said amusingly, 'If he had not been accompanied by a careful servant, parts of his dress would have been frequently separated in his journeys, by very wide intervals.' These times of forgetfulness afforded his family and friends 'considerable merriment, in which no one partook more heartily than himself'.

Although at times during his sickness Rowland thought his ministry was at an end, he actually had another eighteen years to live—eighteen years in which to preach the blessed gospel with new energy and a deeper gratitude for the mercies he had enjoyed. As with everything he did, he made the most of these 'extra years'.

15. Still preaching

Although Rowland and his wife were in the twilight of their days, they did not use old age as an excuse for inactivity. When all sorts of engagements weighed Rowland down, Mrs Hill either answered or arranged his correspondence, and thus helped to relieve his anxiety. Their main source of grief was the death of their friends who had served the Lord so faithfully with them. Often, when he was seated in the pulpit and during the hymn before the sermon, he looked sorrowfully around the congregation. After the service, he said to those who dined with him, 'I could not preach this morning; my eye glanced on the places so long occupied by my dear old friends, now filled by strangers. Ah! I must soon be gone myself; Lord, help me to serve you while I live.'

After working as usual in London and Wotton, Rowland, in the late summer and early autumn of 1820, embarked on a long preaching expedition. Wherever he went he described the congregations as 'astonishing' and sometimes for want of room he was obliged to preach in the open air. He felt the power of God on many occasions. In a letter he wrote to Theophilus Jones, who had become the assistant minister at Wotton Tabernacle, he mentioned the blessing that attended his preaching before saying,

I hate dry, doctrinal preaching, without warm, affectionate, and experimental applications. When we feel what we are at, others will feel too; but when our own sham feelings are substituted in the room of real ones, the people will soon detect us, while this false fire will not communicate any real warmth to the heart. It is poor work to attempt to move the mere passions of others, but as our own hearts are divinely influenced by that power which is from above.

Rowland planned to be back in Wotton sometime before the second Sunday in September in order to prepare for a missionary meeting. On his travels he still thought of his garden and wanted John the gardener to gather the lavender as it got ripe 'and some of the ripest of the balm of Gilead'. He was anxious for his people's prayers, 'that I may not be permitted to suffer spiritual decline in my declining days'.

From Manchester, Rowland visited his family in Shropshire and was received 'with the utmost kindness and affection'. He was invited to preach in some of the neighbouring churches and, on account of a pressing invitation to stay longer, was not able to return to Wotton as soon as he had expected. He preached at Stanton Church and at the chapel his family attended and at a church in Wellington. Mrs Hill, in writing to Jones about her husband's preaching, humorously remarked, 'How can he ever bear to preach at such a poor place as Wotton Tabernacle again, after being such a churchman!'

Dramatic effects from Rowland's preaching occurred throughout his ministry. His biographer Edwin Sidney relates one such incident that took place in 1821, when Rowland was preaching at Norwich. About four years later an old woman was taken from that city into the workhouse at Acle. She became ill and Sidney visited her, and found that she was a Christian. He asked her the means by which she was brought into God's kingdom, and she replied, 'Three or four years ago I saw a crowd going along a street in Norwich; I asked where they were going, and they told me to hear the famous preacher called Rowland Hill. I followed them and could scarcely squeeze in; but I heard him, and the Lord blessed that sermon to my soul. I knew nothing of Christ before, but bless the Lord, I know him now.' That old lady died in the full assurance of faith.

Throughout 1821 Rowland's engagements were as numerous as ever. He thought nothing of preaching six or seven times a week, besides meeting his people and attending to the business of societies for benevolent or religious causes. In all this activity his spirits never failed him and his mind was sharp and vigorous. As the years rolled on his understanding of the solemnity and importance of the sacred office increased. In a letter he exclaimed, 'O for more of the Spirit to make us preach spiritually!' The Bible and good books furnished the preacher with materials, he admitted, 'but unless the Lord himself sends down the celestial fire, there can be neither light nor warmth from the very best of these dead materials. Jesus, the Lord and giver of life, keeps all in his own hands, to keep our souls dependent on himself.' Speaking of a young Baptist preacher, whose sermons were full of dry theology, with little or no anointing, he called him 'a sprig of made up divinity, from a cold water academy'.

In the autumn he travelled, for the benefit of the London Missionary Society, to Norwich, Yarmouth and Bury St Edmunds, where he had not been for nearly fifty years. The last time he had visited Bury he met with violent persecution from the world and coolness in the professors of religion. This time he was kindly received, although he appeared solemn and thoughtful. When he saw all sorts of vehicles bringing large numbers of people to hear him, he exclaimed several times, 'What shall I do, a poor sinful unworthy creature, how shall I preach to this people?' A man who overheard him remarked, 'I am surprised, sir, that you should be so much agitated; I could never have supposed that you felt in this way.' Rowland responded, 'I always feel a great deal before I preach, but I am unusually agitated tonight.'

The place where he was to preach could not contain all who wanted to hear him and hundreds stood outside. The size of the crowd seemed to increase Rowland's excitement. His sermon was taken from Psalm 2:8 and when giving out his text he placed peculiar emphasis on the first word—Take. One who heard him remarked, 'In the whole discourse there was an elevated and sublime range of ideas, and a simplicity and majesty of language, which arrested the attention and astonished the minds of the whole audience. The part of the application, in which he appealed to his hearers on attending to the duty, and cultivating the spirit of prayer, in imitation of Christ, will never be forgotten.'

As he came down from the pulpit, he took Dewhirst, the minister of the chapel, by the hand and burst into tears, crying, 'Good Mr Dewhirst, O that I could be more useful to souls the little time I have to live.' Some were converted and many others drawn into a deeper and more spiritual devotion. So delighted were the people of Bury with his sermon, that in 1822 they pressed him to return, but he was unable to accept the invitation. He wrote to Dewhirst on the subject. 'What a kind set of people you must have with you at Bury, to make so much of the poor defective services you had from me. How true it must be, that the excellency of the power is not of man, but from the Lord alone; and the more we are enabled to depend on him, the more he will honour that dependence by a glorious manifestation of it to the souls of men.'

Rowland's 'eccentric sallies', as they were termed, and his homely illustrations, often 'contained the most important principles and carried conviction to the heart'. Once, about this time, he was far from happy with his Sunday evening sermon. He appeared confused, and after many ordinary and unconnected observations, exclaimed, 'Some of you may think that I am preaching a rambling sermon; but, oh! if I should be able to reach the heart of a poor rambling sinner, you will forgive me. Sinner, you may ramble from Christ, but we will ramble after you, and try and bring you back into his fold.' Just as these remarks were made, a pickpocket entered the chapel, and the words he heard struck his mind powerfully. He returned home deeply affected and destroyed a variety of stolen goods he had prepared for circulation. He spoke several times to Rowland, who 'entertained a firm hope that he was truly converted to God'. Rowland supplied him with many useful household articles and did all he could to restore him into society.

The following year he was engaged to preach one Sunday morning in a small country town more than a hundred miles from London. He had never preached there before. About an hour before the start of the service, a minister told him that several thousands of people would be present, for crowds were pouring in from the surrounding neighbourhood. With an indescribable look on his face, he replied, 'Ah sir, they are coming together, as they think to hear some of my nonsense, but by the help of God they shall not have a sentence of it.' He kept his word, and the sermon was 'remarkable for its deep-toned solemnity'.

In his seventy eighth year, Rowland prepared to make another arduous journey to collect money on behalf of the Missionary Society, which was sinking for want of support. The society had told him that no minister, who travelled to 'beg for them', put them to less expense and collected as much money for them as he did. He was planning to set off on 13 May, after the missionary meeting, and to travel as far as York, some 200 miles, taking in Lincoln, Hull and several other large towns on his way there and back. Although at his time of life he might have been slowing down and taking life more easily, he acknowledged that these later itinerations were 'attended with abundant indications of the power of God to the souls of men, and ... proved times of general refreshment from the presence of the Lord'.

Before he set off his eye became inflamed again and his journey was postponed until 10 June, from which time he preached every day until the 11 July. The congregations and collections were huge, but preaching every day in very hot weather weakened his bodily strength and depressed his spirits. In one of his letters, he ended by saying, 'O how hard I have been worked. Thousands attend field preaching. Frequently almost tired. Still I am upheld, though I was seriously ill.'

On his return to Wotton he wrote about his illness and recovery in a letter to John Wilson, who with many others was worried that his exertions might cause him lasting damage. 'The attack upon my constitution, while it lasted, was certainly very severe. The spasms were so excruciating that had I not been favoured with an attentive servant just at hand, I might have suffered much more severely than I did.' Although the pain and loss of blood affected him, he was so well treated by an excellent Christian doctor, whom the Lord had provided for him, as to be able to continue his itinerant labours with little interruption. He returned to Wotton 'through mercy in perfect health'.

After his 1822 labours in the country, Rowland was on the eve of his departure to London when he fell and broke one of his ribs and suffered severe bruising. He urged Jones to go and supply his place at Surrey Chapel. When he was feeling a little better he wrote to Jones (his first attempt to use a pen since the accident), although his right arm and shoulder were so exceedingly shaken that it was a major effort for him to lift his arm to the table to hold a pen. He told him how the fractured rib was very uncomfortable, and how the accumulation of phlegm made him cough, causing excessive pain. He could not move from one place to another without the help of others.

When the accident first happened Rowland thought he might be able 'just to creep towards the pulpit, and deliver somewhat like an apology for a sermon', but in this he was disappointed. Some weeks later he was hoping to 'preach two half sermons, and procure others to read and pray'. In a postscript to his wife's letter to Sidney, he wrote, 'Through the mercy of God, I am abundantly better, though still, when in bed, I cannot turn, but as I am turned. O that I may be able to spend the very few remains of my days to his glory, by whom I have hitherto been kept.'

James Sherman, who became Rowland's successor at Surrey Chapel according to the great preacher's 'expressed desire', first preached in that place in 1822. Rowland's first letter to him was from Wotton on 7 December of that year, in which he gave details about his 'serious affliction':

How little we know what a day is to bring forth! When I hinted my intention of visiting Reading, little did I know that, according to the wise and unerring providence of my God, the time of a serious affliction was so near at hand. Walking in a straight, but slippery path, my legs flew from under me, one of my ribs was broken, and my whole frame was severely bruised. By this I became as helpless as a child; and still am so disabled as that it is but just in my power to walk from room to room; and though, through mercy on the recovery, I am better, I cannot ascertain how far I am to be kept from my return to my Master's work. By this you may judge how incapable I am of making any promises of future labours and designs.

Rowland slowly recovered from his broken rib and started 1823 with more activity than ever, and there was hardly a day when he was in London that he could call his own. The more he had to do, the happier he appeared.

In December, the poet Southey visited Surrey Chapel and heard Rowland preach. He gave the following interesting description of what he saw and heard:

Rowland Hill's pulpit is raised very high; and before it, at about half the height, is the reader's desk on his right, and the clerk's on his left—the clerk being a very grand personage with a sonorous voice. The singing was so general and so good that I joined in it...

Rowland, a fine tall man, with strong features, very like his portrait, began by reading three verses for his text, stooping to the book in a very peculiar manner. Having done this, he stood erect, and said, 'Why, the text is a sermon, and a very weighty one too.' I could not always follow his delivery, the loss of his teeth rendering his words sometimes indistinct, and the more so, because his pronunciation is peculiar, generally giving *e* the sound of *ai*, like the French. His manner was animated and striking, sometimes impressive and dignified, always remarkable; and so powerful a voice I have rarely or never heard. Sometimes he took off his spectacles, frequently stooped down to read a text, and on these occasions, he seemed to double his body, so high did he stand. He told one or two familiar stories, and used some odd expressions, such as, 'A murrain on those who preach that, when we are sanctified, we do not grow in grace!' And again, 'I had almost said I had rather see the devil in the pulpit than an Antinomian.' The purport of his sermon was good; nothing fanatical, nothing enthusiastic; and the Calvinism it expressed was so qualified as to be harmless. The manner, that of a performer as great in his line as Kean or Kemble; and the manner it is which has attracted so large a congregation about him, all of the better order of persons in business.

In the spring of 1824 he was as busy as ever. His wife in a letter dated 16 March, said, 'Mr Hill is gone into the city on business, and from thence to Hackney to preach. In short, he has so much to do, that I am astonished his strength holds out; but I desire to be thankful for the wonderful health he has.'

16. Four ladies

Rowland enjoyed an affectionate and respectful relationship with his wife, who was raised from obscurity by William Jay in his funeral sermon on her husband. Jay was astonished that 'so little notice had been taken of her', and added this beautiful description of her:

She was a truly gracious woman, of a very sound understanding, and possessing the ornament of a meek and quiet spirit, which is in the sight of God of great price. She was formed for a minister's wife by her prudence, peaceableness, untalkative temper, and unintermeddling conduct. She was singularly suited to the man she espoused; and our friend's obligation to those properties in her character which tended to qualify the peculiarities of his own, were great; and I have no doubt but he would have been willing to say of her, as Mr Newton did of his wife, 'I never followed her advice, but I had reason to approve of it; and I never acted against it, but I had cause to repent of it.'

Mrs Hill was relaxed and affable to those who knew her, but she tended to be distant and reserved with strangers. At times, because of the numbers of people who demanded her husband's attention, she felt it necessary to protect him from imposition or intrusion, which was interpreted by some as rudeness.

Once, when Rowland was taking the funeral of a minister's wife, a friend remarked to him, 'I am afraid our dear minister loved his wife too well; and the Lord, in wisdom, has removed her.' 'What, sir!' exclaimed Rowland, no doubt thinking of his own wife. 'Can a man love a good wife too much? Impossible, sir, unless he can love her better than Christ loves the church. "Husbands, love your wives, even as Christ also loved the church, and gave himself for it."' Mrs Hill always found her husband's 'demeanour in relative and private life perfectly correspondent with his character in official and public life'.

In December 1824, Mrs Hill underwent a serious operation for breast cancer, from which she recovered rapidly, even beyond the expectations of the surgeons, Sir William Blizard and Mr English, who attended her. During her sickness and operation her mind was calm and she was able to look to God for support and courage. When the surgeons were about to strap her down, she begged them to leave her alone, feeling confident that she would be able to sustain the trial. 'Without a struggle or a groan, she endured the terrible operation.' Rowland, on the other hand, was in 'restless agony, until assured that his dear sufferer had passed the ordeal'. In a letter to James Sherman, he gave further details of his wife's trial.

The sufferings of my wife have been exceedingly severe from an operation performed upon her on Wednesday last, by the surgeon's knife, which has deprived her of the whole of her breast, that she might be preserved from certain death from a fast-growing cancer, which soon would have deprived her most painfully of life. Though she bore the operation most patiently, and seems to recover rapidly, I dare not, for the present, speak positively, though I thus drop the hint.

Mrs Hill, writing to her friend, Mrs Edward Walker, explained how her 'five weeks' retirement' had been a time of 'consideration and examination'. 'I cannot look back,' she wrote, 'on *a well spent life*, but, on the contrary, I find much, very much, to mourn over: yet I hope it has, in some measure, been a season of prayer and praise, and that I would not have been without the affliction.'

In 1825 Rowland went through his usual routine in London and then embarked on a journey to the west of England, in the hope that he might prove a blessing to others. He sometimes exclaimed, 'Lord, help me to do a little more good before I die, and raise up young ministers, who shall work from the bottom of their hearts.' While in Bristol, Rowland visited Hannah More for a few hours and both servants of God delighted in one another's company. More's kind friend, Miss Frowd, who was then resident in the house, gave a wonderful portraiture of this meeting:

You cannot imagine how delighted we were with dear old Rowland; instead of a coarse, quaint being, disposed to deal out his witty sarcasms against all, however good, who were not of his *particular genus*, we found a mild mellowed Christian, of a liberality which really astonished us! He quite overflowed with amiable and truly pious conversation, and this was so seasoned with point, humour, and a delightful oddity which was all his own, that we were beyond measure entertained as well as edified by his company, and it made the three hours he spent with us, appear no more than half an hour. He talked with cordial love of Wilberforce, and spoke very highly of

Hannah More

Archbishop Magee. He is an excellent hater of Antinomian doctrines, and I was glad to see such a soundness of Christian principle in the good old man. Upon the question being put to him, 'How many persons he had vaccinated with his own hand?' Mrs M. said, 'I have heard so many as six thousand.' 'Yes, Madam,' he replied, 'nearer eight thousand.' We talked of everybody, from John Bunyan to John Locke, and he really showed an excellent discrimination and tact in character. But the most beautiful feature of all was the spirit of love and charity which was eminently conspicuous in this Christian veteran. I cannot express to you how interesting a spectacle it was to see these two already half-beautified servants of their common Lord, greeting one another for the first, and probably the last time on this side [of] Jordan, preparatory to the consummation of an union and friendship which will last for ever in the regions of eternal felicity. I suppose that no two persons, in their own generation, have done more good in their *respective ways* than Hannah More and Rowland Hill. Both have exceeded fourscore; both retain health and vigour of intellect; both are on the extreme verge of eternity, waiting for the glorious summons, 'Come, ye blessed of my Father.' He concluded this very interesting visit with a fine prayer, which was poured forth in an excellent voice and manner. I really don't know that upon any occasion I have been more gratified.

Chapter 16

Rowland often used to speak of his visit to Hannah More with great enthusiasm, and one of the first things he did was to send his new friend a present. For some time he had been making 'toys' for the children of his friends, instead of reading, which was seriously curtailed by his inflamed eye. His toys were boxes covered with coloured paper, with the letters of the alphabet in partitions, from which sentences and texts from the Bible could be formed. In each box there were directions in easy verse to be learnt by the children and a couplet in rhyme on every letter. Often before breakfast he was seen cutting out the letters, which had been stuck on pasteboard, and carefully sorting them. He sent one of these boxes to Hannah More, whom he regarded as 'so warm and kind a patroness of early education', with a letter and some tracts he had recently published.

More was delighted with her gift and wrote to Rowland from Barley Wood. She 'expressed herself in playful commendation of the easy rhymes contained in the boxes'.

I admire the usefulness and humility of all your baby manufactures; your carefully sorted alphabets are like Ajax making bows and arrows for little children… I like your poetry even more than your prose… The penalty imposed on the loser of a letter, and the skilful division of the letters of the alphabet, is a novelty in the art of poetry which I suppose Horace omitted, that he might leave you the credit of the invention.

Rowland also made tiny shoes for babies and would sometimes promise his female friends that when they got married he would be happy to present 'the first-born' with a pair of nursery slippers. He followed a pattern of the various parts from which he cut out the shoe and then sewed them together very neatly. These little shoes were highly valued by his friends who were fortunate enough to own a pair.

At this time a Miss Sheppard, a young lady living at Ridge near Uley in Gloucestershire, offered to paint his portrait, with the view of building an infant school from the profits of the sale of a print engraved from her painting. Rowland agreed. An interesting correspondence subsequently occurred between Rowland and Miss Sheppard, and in the first note Rowland, in reference to the painting, said, 'It certainly must be the universal opinion, that you have *hit me off* very correctly.' Miss Sheppard wanted Rowland to promote the sale of the engraving, but he felt awkward about trying to 'sell a representation of myself', and hoped his wife could 'do what I cannot'. A further difficulty he envisaged was that the customers had 'shallow pockets and short purses' and 'generally complain of want of money for more important purposes', but he hoped the 'effort may be made with some little success'.

In a further letter to Miss Sheppard, Rowland commented that he was prepared to exhibit the print of the painting in the hope of picking up 'some customers for the accomplishment of [her] kind design'. However, he was not very hopeful as his people were poor and found it necessary to 'seek after cheap bargains'. As always he took the opportunity to speak of Christ, who alone is the giver of a 'most glorious life to all those who are born from above'.

Rowland's last letter to Miss Sheppard on the subject of the print was written from Surrey Chapel on 7 May 1827. In it he complained of the 'perpetual bustle' of London life and a variety of public meetings and institutions that had taken up too much of his time and energy. He also mentioned another print which was in circulation, which he feared would dull the sale of Miss Sheppard's, at least in the metropolis, especially as it was exhibited at a print shop nearly opposite the chapel.

In spite of the competition, Miss Sheppard's portrait sold sufficiently well for her to be able to lay the foundation stone of a spacious room at Uley in the autumn of 1827, which was opened the following spring. The school housed about 160 infants and fifty girls, and was also used as a Sunday school for 300 children.

Rowland sent one of the portraits to his friend Mrs Lloyd of Bronwydd, Wales, with a humorous letter in the form of a dialogue written on the back, part of which is reproduced below.

'Goodness! [exclaims Mrs Lloyd as she opens the letter] if it is not a print of Mr Hill, as like him as it can stare. But poor old soul, what vanity to send me his picture! Well, well, I must forgive him; perhaps his late illness may have given a little twist to his brains...'

Enter Mrs Williams

Mrs Lloyd—'Madam, did you ever see any one like this? You must not look at the name.'

Mrs Williams—'Let me see, I can't recollect.'

Mrs Lloyd—'Not recollect, look again; think of some old odd minister.'

Mrs Williams—'Bless me, if it is not Mr Rowland Hill, and how like it is!—only I think they have made him a little too broad about the shoulders. But where will you hang him, madam?'

Mrs Lloyd—'Why there is the difficulty. I can't think of putting such a little bit of a pimping print in the best room, it will look so odd a contrast to the others.'

Mrs Williams—'Suppose, madam, you were to hang him up in one of the closets belonging to the best bedchamber.'

Mrs Lloyd—'I shall not like to hang the queer old creature so much out of my sight as all that. I should like now and then to have a peep at him, that I may be reminded of some of his comical speeches when I am low.'

Mrs Williams—'Suppose, then, madam, you were to hang him up in the housekeeper's room.'

Mrs Lloyd—'A good thought, that is just the place for him; there are several prints of old statesmen and warriors, and among the rest is a smoke dried worm eaten print of some bishop. I think that frame will just do it. He can't be affronted if he succeeds a bishop. I'll ring for Mrs Davis, and tell her to bring the frame.'

Even in his old age Rowland lost none of his wit and charm. As far as succeeding a bishop was concerned, he often said that the only preferment he would take in the church was a bishopric; he did not think he could resist that office!

In the spring of 1827 he visited Brighton and parts of Kent and Sussex. He also worked hard in London before embarking on his proposed preaching tour of South Wales, where, inspired by the beauty of his surroundings, he seemed to throw off the weaknesses of old age. 'He both caught and imparted warmth wherever he went amongst that animated people, and generally returned from his visits to the Principality refreshed both in body and mind.' Charlesworth says that he was followed by huge crowds in Wales, where he 'would seize the opportunity of the noontide rest from labour to gather round him the Welsh peasantry who lived in the mountains, and on summer evenings thousands would congregate on the side of some romantic hill, after a walk of many miles by rugged and steep paths, to listen to his preaching'.

On one of these visits a lady called on him and during the course of the conversation inquired, 'Do you remember preaching at Wrexham, sir, about fifty years ago in a field not far from Peny Bryn?' 'Oh yes,' replied Rowland, 'I remember the time very well.' Both parties smiled when the lady remarked, 'I see you remember the pigs, sir!' 'Indeed I do—and never shall forget them.' After they had laughed together about the past, the lady said, 'I was then very young, and was led by curiosity to hear you preach, and I hope the word then came with power to my soul.' The incident that had made the service unforgettable was as follows:

Near the spot where he preached there was a tenter field, on which a fine kind of thread or yarn was exposed to the air. Several women, who were taking care of it, observing a number of persons assembling together, were tempted to quit their employ for a short season. The gate of the field was left open and several large pigs walked in. In a few moments the intruders got the iron which is pierced through their snouts entangled in the twine; and the more they shook, the more they found themselves imprisoned. The loud cries of the pigs alarmed the women who soon found out the mischief which had been done. They ran to the spot, and a general pursuit took place. Mr Hill, while preaching, observed several of the women falling upon the poor animals, turning them on their backs, and then endeavouring to disentangle their heads from the twine: this trifling event produced considerable amusement, and for a time interfered with the service.

Thomas Jackson, who frequently travelled with Rowland on his tours through Wales, stated that his ministry was remarkably blessed, particularly in the south. The impression from his preaching that was left on the minds of the Welsh was so deep that when he visited Haverfordwest, after an absence of forty years, the people rang the church bells for joy that he was again permitted to visit them. He found several who had been converted under his ministry all those years ago still alive and rejoicing.

17. 'A painful separation'

Towards the end of 1829 Rowland complained of the difficulties caused by his poor eyesight, and on 16 February 1830 he wrote to Sidney, saying that his eyes were so dim through age that he could hardly see to write. The weather was particularly bad that winter and he had been virtually 'kept a prisoner at home' ever since his arrival in town. He then told Sidney how he wished to imitate the style of the apostle Paul, 'I really think, taking him as a whole, a greater man never lived, since his days to the present day.' He wanted to copy that 'wise, that dignified simplicity of speech the apostle used, when he preached the gospel with the Holy Ghost sent down from heaven, which so effectually wrought on the hearts of all them who believed'.

Rowland's eyesight became so bad that for two years before his death he dictated to an amanuensis. However, he was never prevented from preaching the gospel. Mrs Hill told Sidney, 'Mr Hill, notwithstanding a very bad cold, started yesterday for a fortnight's tour in Kent,' and he returned refreshed and much better.

About May, William Jones was talking with Rowland and his wife and the conversation turned to various anecdotes that had been circulated about Rowland. One of these popular stories respected the highwayman who stopped Rowland, only to be so overcome by Christian kindness that he became his coachman and, after living with him for twenty years, died in his service. Rowland assured Jones that the tale did not concern him, but Fothergill. Rowland had merely related the incident in a funeral sermon, which he had preached on the death of a member of his congregation. He once took up a copy of *Percy's Anecdotes*, where the 'fact' was recorded, along with another story equally without foundation, respecting the time he had visited a poor emaciated person, stretched on a miserable bed in a garret and without a shirt. According to the tale, he immediately took off his shirt and gave it to the destitute invalid. Across the first anecdote he wrote 'a lie' and on the other he scribbled 'another lie', and then added his name.

Mrs Hill was listening intently to this conversation and she inquired, with a smile, 'Have you heard anything about me?' Jones told her of the reports of her husband throwing a new cap she had bought him into the fire as soon as it arrived home; of his assertion in chapel, 'Here comes Mrs Hill with a chest of drawers on her head,' referring to her highly fashionable bonnet; and of several other rumours that were current in the country. Both husband and wife declared the tales to be false, and Rowland was upset that such statements should be spread abroad. 'Sir,' said Rowland, with a solemn air, 'I hope that the Christian minister, if not the gentleman, always prevented me from making my wife a laughing stock for the amusement of the vulgar.'

There was another tale that involved Mrs Hill:

One night after [Rowland] had been in bed for some hours, he felt an impulse to get up and take a walk. Wandering into the Strand (which, by the bye, was entirely out of his beat), he was there accosted by an unfortunate woman, with whom he entered into conversation; and finding her, as he thought, weary of her evil course of life, and desirous of turning from it, he took her to his house, and prevailed upon Mrs Hill to receive her as a domestic.

This tale was first told of Edmund Burke and subsequently transferred to Rowland, without any authority.

On one occasion, Jones suggested that, because of so many false stories, it was important that a qualified person should give an authentic version of his life and ministry. Rowland replied, 'What can anyone say about me? A poor unworthy creature, I'm sure. No, I want no life.' Mrs Hill disagreed and expressed her hope that an accurate memoir would be published, especially as she knew of more than one person who was collecting material for that purpose. Rowland nodded his approval.

The operation for breast cancer that Mrs Hill had endured prolonged her life by several years, but her body never fully recovered from the shock. During the spring of 1830, she often expressed a conviction that her earthly pilgrimage was drawing to a close, a premonition that came true soon after her departure from London. Her health suddenly deteriorated during the summer, and continued to decline until her death. Probably the last letter she dictated was in the handwriting of Rowland's confidential servant, Charles Goring. It is dated Wotton, 20 July 1830, and addressed to Edwin Sidney. In the letter she said that her health was worse than when she had been in London. She had travelled to Gloucester to consult Dr Barron who was doubtful of her recovery. She felt 'extremely weak' and was scarcely able to go up or down stairs. The doctor had advised her not to go to the sea and to be kept as quiet as possible. At the same time Rowland was 'as well as can be expected'.

At the beginning of August her state of health was so worrying that Rowland wrote to Sidney about her expected death and his own feelings of grief.

I am now passing through deep waters, and I feel myself almost overwhelmed by them. I fear the increasing debility, which of late has been making a rapid progress upon Mrs Hill's constitution, will soon terminate in her dissolution... Considering her natural timidity, she is as calm as can be expected; but O the solemn stroke of death! The thoughts of such a separation sink my spirits exceedingly. I would still try to labour, but under such burdened spirits, how difficult the task! While the feelings of human nature cannot, and indeed should not altogether be resisted, yet still it is [our] duty to say, 'The Lord gave, and the Lord hath taken away; blessed be the name of the Lord.'

In a postscript Rowland discouraged Sidney from paying a visit because of his wife's extreme weakness.

Five days after the above letter was written, on 17 August 1830, at Wotton, Mrs Hill crossed the river to her eternal home. Rowland's grief was so acute that he left all the funeral arrangements to his friend Theophilus Jones. Although he was finding writing a 'burdensome task' and had employed a substitute to perform this task, on his birthday, 23 August, the day before his wife's funeral, he wrote to his niece,

I wish submissively to say, 'The Lord gave, the Lord hath taken away, blessed be the name of the Lord,' but I have felt it a painful separation after a union of upwards of sixty years. And this day I enter the eighty seventh year of my age, considering the exercise both of body and mind, I have been called to sustain, I am surprised my life has been so long preserved, but it is now most certain that I am now just stepping into the grave... The vault is now opening to receive her remains, where she is to be deposited on the morrow, till the trumpet shall sound and the dead shall be raised and we shall be changed. O for a still better change, a divine change of heart that we may be prepared for that most solemn day.

In spite of his grief, he managed to preach his wife's funeral sermon from Romans 8:28, and in noticing her character and fortitude, he suddenly exclaimed:

Do you remember my preaching in those fields, by the old stump of the tree? The multitude was great, and many were disposed to be riotous. At first I addressed them firmly; but when a desperate gang of banditti drew near, with the most ferocious looks and horrid imprecations and menaces, my courage began to fail. My wife was then standing behind me, as I stood on the table. I think I hear her now. She pulled my gown (he then put his hand behind him, and touched his gown), and, looking up, said, 'George, play the man for your God.' My confidence returned. I again spoke to the multitude with boldness and affection; they became still; and many were deeply affected.

Soon after the funeral Rowland wrote to Sidney and said that 'though the innocent aberrations of her mind, during the last few days of her life, were somewhat painful, and drew many a tear from my eyes, yet, at collected intervals, she would be in a state of fervent ejaculatory prayer'.

Rowland wrote to his friend Henry Brooker of Brighton, a man who had sustained a similar loss and who had shown him tender sympathy.

It could not but be supposed, that after a union of [nearly] sixty years, a separation must have been severely felt. Though for some weeks before Mrs Hill's departure I was prepared for the stroke, yet when the solemn event really took place, I found that anticipation proved but a feeble defence of what afterwards I was called to feel. You had once the same sharp trial to sustain, and I am sure, after such a trial as you were called to undergo, nature must have had hard struggles in you before you could say meekly, 'Thy will be done.' To live without natural affection converts a man into a monster.

Rowland and his wife had been joined by a deep and affectionate bond, and their opposite personalities blended together in a godly partnership. What was wanting in one was generally supplied by the other. 'Gifted with a sound and discriminating judgement, Mrs Hill managed with peculiar tact the difficult task of controlling her husband's ardent nature, without checking his usefulness or activity; and the weight of her influence was so nicely balanced, that it restrained but did not repress, it wisely directed but did not dictate.' She understood that she was married to a preacher of the gospel, and not once during their marriage did she allow personal convenience or inclination to interrupt his service to God. Naturally she was reserved and hard to get to know, but those who became her friends never forgot her sincerity and solid though retiring qualities of mind. Thomas Jackson called her a 'mother in Israel; her sterling piety, her good sense, and her very liberal attention to the temporal wants of the poor ... endeared her to persons of every class, and her name will long live in the grateful recollection of those who partook of her bounty'.

Rowland was beginning to feel more acutely the effects of old age and his poor eyesight was a real hindrance. His wife had helped him greatly in arranging his extensive correspondence; but after her death he was compelled to rely on his servant. One of his letters started with a little poem: 'Charles must write while I indite, for lack of sight, by candlelight!'

Only sixteen days after his wife's death, he wrote to W. Rice, a member of the open communion Baptist church in Northampton, who had invited him up to preach. After mentioning how God's people 'should all of them look upon themselves as one in Christ Jesus; and the more we have of his loving spirit, the more we shall "love one another with pure hearts fervently"'; he referred to the 'very painful event' that had kept him 'a prisoner at this place. I could not leave my late dear companion in life during her last declining days.' Since her departure, letters of kind condolence had been sent 'from every quarter' and he was planning to answer them all.

When Rowland returned to London in November he was very reserved in reference to his bereavement and said little about his feelings. He was often reticent to talk about those things that affected him personally. However, it was obvious to all that his sorrow was heartfelt. The lonely room and the vacated chair made him sometimes 'groan being burdened'. He wanted to refer to her last days in a sermon on the text: 'We know that if the earthly house of this tabernacle were dissolved, we have a building of God, a house not made with hands, eternal in the heavens.' Soon after he had started to preach, he distantly touched on his bereavement, but was unable to continue, and exclaimed in tears, 'Oh! it is painful work to be separated from a dear friend after a happy union of nearly sixty years.'

18. 'Outwardly wasting away'

About three years before Rowland's own death, the following interesting incident occurred. Two men entered Surrey Chapel, one of whom was a godless man about to leave for India. After many prayers for his salvation, his Christian friend had persuaded him to spend his four last Sunday evenings in church. On the first three Sundays the sermons in the various churches they attended were listened to with polite interest but no impression was made on the mind of the 'wanderer'. On the last Sunday, the Christian was deeply burdened for his friend's soul and so took him to Surrey Chapel to hear 'good Rowland Hill'. He secretly prayed that the preacher might be in a serious mood and not indulge in any eccentric remarks. Rowland gave out his text, 'We are not ignorant of his devices,' and immediately told the following story:

Many years since, I met a drove of pigs in one of the streets of a large town, and to my surprise they were not driven, but quietly followed their leader. This singular fact excited my curiosity, and I pursued the swine, until they all quietly entered the butchery. I then asked the man how he succeeded in getting the poor, stupid, stubborn pigs so willingly to follow him; when he told me the secret. He had a basket of beans under his arm, and kept dropping them as he proceeded, and so secured his object.

Ah! my dear hearers, the devil has got his basket of beans, and he knows how to suit his temptations to every sinner. He drops them by the way—the poor sinner is thus led captive by the devil at his own will; and if the grace of God prevent not, he will get him at last into his butchery, and there he will keep him for ever. Oh, it is because 'we are not ignorant of his devices', that we are anxious this evening to guard you against them!

The Christian friend was upset that Rowland had told this tale about the pigs, fearing his unbelieving companion would chuckle to himself rather than feel any conviction in his mind and heart. After the service, they left the chapel together and for a while all was silent. 'What a singular statement we had tonight about the pigs, and yet how striking and convincing it was!' remarked the unbeliever. His mind was so impressed that he could not forget the basket of beans, the butchery and the final loss of the sinner's soul. He travelled to India and corresponded with his friend, and continually referred to this sermon as having produced a deep and abiding impression on his mind.

Rowland Hill as an old man

Occasionally Rowland's age, loneliness and physical weaknesses caused him to feel 'cast down, though not destroyed'. He once sent for William Jones, who found him in 'deep despondency of spirit'. Jones stayed with him the whole afternoon. Rowland's mental anxiety was so great that he was not able to preach and a friend occupied his pulpit in the evening. When Jones returned to him after the service, he found him cheerful and at peace, and he put his despondency down to the state of his body and the recent loss of his wife. Sometimes the glorious and majestic character of God seemed almost too much for him to bear and he would say with awe, 'Behold, I am vile.' An old friend once asked if he enjoyed the comforts of assurance. He replied, with a deep confidence in his Saviour, 'I cannot say that I have much joy,—I have no triumphs,—but my mind is immovably fixed on the glorious atonement of Christ; there I rest.'

He was delivered out of one bout of depression by an amusing letter. His servant entered the room with the letter, which required an answer.

'Charles, read the letter,' said Rowland. It stated that the writer was the child of godly parents in Lincolnshire, who had brought him up in the training and instruction of the Lord. On his coming to London, where he stayed for only a few days, he had fallen in with bad companions who, while he was asleep, had stolen all his clothes. He was therefore forced to remain in bed until he could borrow clothes in the neighbourhood. In the letter he appealed to Rowland for help, on the grounds that 'his parents had heard him preach in the county'. Rowland was greatly amused by the story and laughed heartily over it. His depression lifted and for the rest of the evening he enjoyed much serenity of mind.

Thankfully the dark times did not last long, and he was usually in a lively humour. On one occasion during this period, William Jones called on Rowland and saw that he was talking with a respectable-looking lady. He started to withdraw from the room when Rowland called him back and begged him to be seated. A silence of a few seconds followed and then Rowland gave a sly shrug, which signalled to Jones that the lady was an unwelcome visitor. The silence was soon broken when the lady started to speak to Jones.

'Sir, I have felt it my duty to call on this good old gentleman, and endeavour to explain to him some great truths of which he appears to be quite ignorant. I heard him preach yesterday, and was quite distressed to think the people should be so misled. I have been talking with him, but he does not appear to understand me. Poor gentleman, I suppose his mind is getting very weak.'

'Very weak indeed,' said Mr Hill.

The female teacher then expounded to me her prophetical system, and inquired, 'Do you understand me?'

'No, madam, I do not.'

'Dear me, how dark are the minds of some of the Lord's children!'

'There now!' exclaimed my friend, 'you have got it.'

I did not attempt to answer the rhapsody of the lady, and received her lecture in humble silence. At length, Mr Hill, in a loud whisper across the table, said, pointing his finger to his head, and looking towards his fair friend, 'I think there's a screw loose.' This was enough for the learned female theologian, and she immediately decamped. 'I love to answer a fool according to her folly,' said Mr Hill; and there the matter ended.

Although Rowland kept his sense of humour till the last, there were signs in his old age of a more serious contemplation of the world to come. He often sat silently in the window of his dining room, speaking out scriptural expressions and sometimes, when a thought struck him, he would turn his reflection into verse. He was not altogether delivered from the fear of death and 'rejoiced with trembling' at the thought of the great change. He once said, with the most solemn feelings, 'Even the apostle says, "The last enemy that shall be destroyed is death." Yes, he is an enemy, but a conquered one to the believer.'

On another occasion he observed, 'There are some people who often talk about looking back on a well spent life. I look up to him who spent his life gloriously to redeem my precious soul; and there alone I dare to look. I thank God who has kept me from the grosser sins of the world, but there is not a prayer more suitable for my dying lips than that of the publican, "God, be merciful to me, a sinner."' For a considerable time before his death his mind contemplated 'the day of his departure', and in his sermons he often shared his thoughts, as well as highlighting the victory of Christ over all things.

In the spring of 1831, as he was getting into his carriage after one of the meetings at Exeter Hall, he grazed his leg against the step. It stung a little, but he took no further notice of it. After a few days it started to swell painfully and he was confined to the house for some time. In May he wrote to Thomas Bull at Newport Pagnel, and said,

During the missionary week I grazed my shin bone; the injury, however, appeared so trifling, that I did not suppose I should be interrupted in my previous engagements; though I have waited till the last moment, yet the increased inflammation deprives me of all hopes of being able to accomplish my intended journey. I am forbidden by my surgeon all sorts of exercise and exertions; and if I transgress, the result is immediately against me.

Chapter 18

By Thursday 2 June, the wound in his leg appeared better, so he left London for Leamington and, as he went by easy stages, he was able to preach once on the Sunday. He found things in an unsettled state and the anxiety he suffered caused his injury to become inflamed again. However, he preached on the following Tuesday, which increased his sufferings to such an extent that he was confined to his room for many days.

On 2 August he wrote from Wotton to W. D. Wills, one of the managers of the Tabernacle at Bristol, a place of happy memories for Rowland, whose bodily weakness is clear from the letter.

During the last winter I have been visited with such an inflammation in one of my eyes, that I can scarcely see what I write, nor can I read the plainest printed chapter in the Bible but with difficulty, unless by a previous recollection of its contents; add to this, an injury done to the shin bone during the missionary week has greatly crippled me, while a small open wound still continues to demand attention and care. I am at length compelled to have a young friend with me to attend to the short services belonging to this place alone, while a few efforts occasionally, to serve some of the smaller congregations in the vicinage, seems to be the utmost my exhausted strength will admit...

While I am obliged to cease from what is called labour, may I wait with holy patience for my eternal rest in Christ. That day, with me, I am now sure, is very near at hand. That gospel which I have preached I may say many thousands of times to others, is now the only solid resting place of my soul: though in this letter I scarcely see what I write, yet in this I feel what I write. Though I don't lament over what I have preached, yet I greatly lament that I have not preached the same truths with more spirituality, fervour and devotedness of heart. Though I cannot charge myself as having been a lazy drone, yet, as a busy bee, oh! that I had been better taught how to collect the sacred honey from those hills from whence all our hopes of salvation come.

His leg troubled him throughout the autumn, at the end of which he went to Leamington, where a surgeon was able to help him to such a degree that he recovered rapidly. He returned to London at the end of the year somewhat renewed and was able to preach once a Sunday during the winter.

These physical problems had seriously weakened his constitution, but his mind was as active and alert as ever. He loved to use anecdotes to drive home the point he was making. In one sermon he said,

I remember that many years ago, in the country, a good old lady used to stand behind my pulpit, a clergyman's widow, and a very excellent character. She was very deaf, and she used to put her [ear-] trumpet almost under my mouth, and catch now and then a word; she would then take away the trumpet, and lay it aside, and pray to God to send down a blessing on that word; and then she would put up her trumpet again, and try to get another word, and that word would excite another prayer. She could hear but few words, but had many a blessing conveyed into her heart from the few words that she could hear. *You* have got ears to hear *all* that I say; but oh! That God the Holy Spirit would come down that hearing might be the least part of it. May our Gospel, when it comes to you, come to the spirit, 'not in word only, but in power'.

Rowland left London early in May and, although in general excellent health and alert mentally, he was weaker physically than he had ever been. On the day of his departure he asked William Jones to attend to some small commissions, and so Jones was with him a few minutes before he left the chapel house. Having finished his lunch, Rowland called out, 'Charles, are the horses ready?' 'Not quite, sir,' replied Charles the servant. Jones described what followed as 'the most interesting scene [I] ever witnessed in connection with Mr Hill':

'Horses are good things,' Rowland remarked. 'I had one that carried me many miles to preach the gospel; he was a kind creature; I remember I taught him to dance, and he managed it very well indeed. Oh! me—I am now leaving this place, never, perhaps, to see it again. Oh! it is a solemn thought. Charles, where is the old cat? I've not seen him for a long time; he used to keep my feet warm in the winter, and curl his tail round my legs.

'How does Doctor—go on? I don't much like that man. There's something odd about him, and his temper is queer. Charles, are the horses ready?'

'Nearly so, sir.'

'I had a cow once at Wotton, and she was a great favourite; I tried to teach her to dance, but, poor thing! she made a sad [?] out of it. I once permitted her to give me a ride, but I had no sooner got on her back, than away she went, quite delighted with her load, but I was soon upset; so I never gave her another treat.'

At this point Charles entered and said, 'The horses are ready, sir.' 'Oh! dear, *must* I go?' He rose with difficulty from his chair, walked over to the door and, turning back, sighed and looked closely round the room. Then, in a subdued tone, with his eyes raised, he exclaimed, 'Oh! it is a solemn thought—I am not likely to see this place again.' He paused and in a voice a little louder than a whisper, added, 'But what a mercy to have lived here fifty years, and by heavenly grace to have been kept unspotted from the world!' He then slowly climbed down the steps into the kitchen, where the servants were waiting to say goodbye. Standing in the middle of the room, he said with deep emotion, 'You'll not see your old master again,' which caused everyone in the kitchen to burst into tears.

Just at that moment, the old cat appeared. 'You nasty old creature,' said Rowland, 'so you have just come to say mew, mew, before I go: where have you been? ah! you may mew. Let me stroke his back, Daniel.' The cat was picked up and Rowland, having patted him several times, ordered him to be set free, and off he ran. Rowland then walked to the coach yard. He looked for a second or two with deep interest at the chapel, and said, 'There I have preached for fifty years; but my work is done.' He climbed into the carriage and exclaimed as he drew up the window blind, 'Farewell, till bodies meet to part no more.' He retired to Wotton, for the last time.

19. The last enemy

The first sermon that Rowland preached in 1833 was on 6 January, and it contained emotional and prophetic allusions to his own death, which was only three months away.

Many of my friends [he remarked] have been swept away by the scythe of time into eternity since this time twelve months; and there is one standing among you now who does not expect to see this year out. The days of my pilgrimage must be nearly ended... Oh, it is beautiful to see the setting sun on a summer's day—though the rays are faint, yet they are still bright and clear. So while the rays of my poor abilities begin to get very feeble, God can still give a light to them—I pray that he may be a light and life to your souls.

Rowland Hill as a very old man

Further on in the same sermon he remembered

...once seeing an old man, I suppose he must have been seventy or eighty years of age; and I asked him how old he was. He looked at me (he was brought to me as a monument of mercy), he looked at me for a time, and faltered in his voice, the tears trickling down his cheeks; says he, 'I am two years old.' 'Two years old?' 'Ah, Sir,' says he, 'till a little time ago I lived the life of a dead man; and I never knew what life was till I met with the life which is "hid with Christ in God".' Oh, it is a glorious truth; we have a life in God.

Not long before his death Rowland met an aged acquaintance and joked, 'If you and I don't march off soon, our friends yonder will think we have missed our way.' On a separate occasion, in reference to the peace he felt in the light of death, he said, 'It is a great mercy to have a soft pillow under our head in a dying hour; but to enjoy this privilege, remember we must live near to God.'

His increasing weakness prevented him in the first weeks of 1833 from preaching, except once every Sunday in Surrey Chapel and then he had to be supported by an elevated but uncomfortable seat in the pulpit. The ladies in the congregation, realising his difficulty, presented him with a more comfortable chair, with an appropriate and respectful letter, to which he replied with heartfelt thanks.

He was constantly thinking about appointing his successor at Surrey Chapel and on one occasion he mentioned his intention of writing to a clergyman, who had conscientious scruples about remaining in the church. 'Do you know him, sir; they tell me he's a nice lad.' 'No, sir,' replied William Jones, with tongue in cheek, 'but I understand he has been a neighbour of yours for a considerable time.' 'A neighbour of mine, sir, where does he live?' asked Rowland somewhat surprised. 'Within the walls of the King's Bench prison!' 'Mercy on us, we must not write to him, however.'

In his sermon for 3 March he mentioned how some years before a poor youth had come to Surrey Chapel.

He had been very wicked, and he said he came here to hear a man who was looked on as being something out of the way (and he is very fond of being out of the way, that he may catch others who are out of the way); however, he came to the place, and went home broken-hearted, and he said to his brother, 'Oh, brother, if you had been where I have been today, you would have felt what I did. We have been very wicked; O come and hear the man I have been hearing, and see what he has got to say to your soul.' The brothers both came, 'and nobody can tell,' said the young man, 'the joyous feelings of my heart when I looked into my brother's face, and saw the penitential tears begin to trickle down his face.' O try and bring your relatives and friends to hear the word of God.

Both these young men became devoted servants of Christ, and were numbered by Rowland as 'worthies', whom he delighted to talk about.

On Sunday 31 March he preached for the last time, his text being 1 Corinthians 2:7 8. Although exceedingly feeble, he preached for nearly fifty minutes. The outline of this sermon was kept and afterwards published by George Weight, whom Rowland had engaged as an assistant minister to help him with his stated functions at Surrey Chapel. It reads rather like a confession of faith as he mentions his conversion when a boy at Eton and the success of his early ministry. His final appeal to the sinner is both typical and striking: 'How will you escape, if you neglect so great a salvation? You say you hope to come to Christ by and by. By and bys are not with you; you may be struck dead before your by and bys come. God be praised, we can say, "His arm is not shortened that it cannot save;" it is stretched out, even now.'

He felt so well that he engaged to preach again the following Tuesday evening (2 April) to the teachers of the Southwark Sunday School Union, but became so weak on that day that he was obliged to ask his assistant, Mr Weight, to officiate for him, promising to add a few words if he was able. After Weight's short sermon, Rowland climbed into the pulpit with great difficulty and delivered, 'with unusual fervour and animation', a brief (fifteen minutes) and affectionate address, in which he told those who heard him how he 'rejoiced still to feel his heart in the work'. He left the pulpit completely exhausted. This was his last effort.

Although he was extremely weak, he intended to preach on Good Friday, and it was only the intervention of Weight that kept him from the pulpit that day. At breakfast he had complained of 'excessive languor' and therefore was encouraged to remain in the house during the morning service. He had planned to preach from Hebrews 10:4, but instead asked Weight to apologize to the congregation, saying, 'I cannot now do the things that I would: I hope I am not a lazy minister, though I am compelled to be an inactive one.' At about one o'clock he went for a ride in his carriage towards Camberwell, but did not return as refreshed as he had hoped. He stayed downstairs all day and talked freely with all who visited him. During the evening he suffered a 'temporary aberration of mind', but it soon passed. A surgeon came and said that Rowland's 'temporal arteries were distended and threatened apoplexy'. He was so successfully treated that the next morning he rose at his usual hour in good spirits and ate a hearty breakfast. He passed the day comfortably and in the evening the newspapers were read to him. He thought of preaching on the Sunday and had already chosen his text, 1 Peter 1:3, but he was not well enough. Instead, he spent the day in tolerable comfort and sat up until ten o'clock at night.

On Easter Monday, Rowland said to Thomas Jackson, 'If it had pleased God to have taken me to himself while I was at Wotton, I should have liked to have been buried with Mrs Hill; but, as my heavenly Father has otherwise determined, I would rather be buried in Surrey Chapel, where I have preached for half a century, than have my body carried so many miles after my death.'

During Tuesday evening of Easter week Rowland's servant, Charles, noticed such a change in his master that he informed Lord Hill. Unfortunately his lordship was out of town, but his nephew and aid de camp, Captain George Hill, immediately attended him and brought with him his uncle's doctor, who thought Rowland was dying, but because of the 'great strength of constitution he might rally for a short time', which turned out to be a forlorn hope.

On Wednesday evening, Rowland's mental lapses were 'at times very painful' on account of disease, but when his mind did not wander it was drawn to heavenly things. On one of these occasions he called for his servant and asked him to read 2 Corinthians 5. At the fourth verse, he looked up and said, 'Ah, Charles, we do not like to die!' and at the seventeenth verse he exclaimed in a strong tone, 'A new existence, mind that! Ah, Charles, I shall soon leave you!' About ten that night he called for Weight to conduct family prayers by his bedside, refusing to rest until he had concluded. During the night his servant heard him cry out, 'How soon will thy seat of judgement appear, prepare me to meet and welcome thee there.'

George Clayton was allowed to visit his friend right up to the end, and he has given this account of his closing conversation with Rowland:

I was at his bedside within a few hours of his dissolution: it was truly an impressive scene. Lord Hill's physician was with him when I arrived, and remarked that nothing more could be attempted for the venerable patient, and the expected change must soon take place. Mr Hill grasped my hand with much affection, and said, 'You have often seen me ill, and I recovered; but this is an irrecoverable complaint, I shall not get over it—it is a solemn thing to die. I have no rapturous joys, but peace—a good hope through grace—all through grace.'

Jackson, who was also in the room, observed, 'You would not give up the hope you have, sir, for all the world.' 'No,' said Rowland firmly, '*not for ten thousand thousand worlds.* Christ is everything to a dying man— but I want to be perfectly holy—perfectly like my dear Lord—without holiness there is no such thing as getting to heaven.' After this he roused himself and said strongly, 'The greatest curse that ever entered the church of God is dirty antinomianism.' Both men, finding him exhausted, prayed for him and then left him alone.

On Thursday phlegm in his chest prevented him from speaking very clearly, but Weight heard him softly repeating verses of Scripture and hymns, particularly, 'Eye hath not seen, nor ear heard, neither hath entered into the heart of man, the things that God hath prepared for them that love him;' and 'Christ also hath once suffered for sins, the just for the unjust, that he might bring us unto God.' About ten o'clock that morning, Weight gently whispered to him those favourite lines from the Moravian Bishop Gambold's hymn, which were almost hourly on Rowland's lips:

And when I'm to die,
Receive me, I'll cry,
For Jesus hath lov'd me, I cannot say why—
But this, I can find,
We two are so join'd,
He'll not be in glory, and leave me behind.

Rowland tried to utter them, but could not. This was the last evidence of sensibility he gave. He gradually became weaker and about twenty five minutes to six on Thursday evening, 11 April 1833, without a sound or a struggle, he slipped into the presence of his Lord, whom he had served so faithfully for so long. Those around could hardly believe he had gone so peaceful was his end, but this tranquil passing was an answer to his own prayers.

The announcement of his death was felt deeply by his people, many of whom had been baptised by him as infants or led to the Saviour through his ministry. They had indeed lost a 'father and a friend'. They were allowed to see his body before it was removed to its final resting place. General Lord Hill, writing to his nephew, said, 'I expect there will be an immense crowd at Surrey Chapel on Friday [the day of Rowland's funeral]; vast numbers of people have been to see the body, the concourse … was so great that the police were obliged to attend.'

Rowland had been a friend and supporter of the Village Itinerancy, or Evangelical Association for the Progress of the Gospel, and he bequeathed the bulk of his property to the treasurer 'for the pious and benevolent uses and purposes of that Association'. This amounted to £11,000. At a meeting of the committee for managing the affairs of the society, held on Wednesday 17 April, two days before Rowland's funeral and before they were informed of his bequest, they drew up a testimonial of their departed friend, in which they said:

We reflect with gratitude on his unbending adherence to the truth as it is in Jesus—on the singular endowments which he possessed—the extensive field of labour which he occupied—the very long and protracted term of more than sixty years spent in the faithful ministry of the gospel—and for a measure of success in the conversion of sinners to a degree unprecedented, as we believe, in our times…

His benevolence was not the effervescence of feeling, it was the product of permanent principle, the grace of the Holy Spirit; steady and active and operative in all the charities of life: in his own house diffusing comfort, order and happiness; in his vicinity extending its tender solicitudes to the poor, the aged, the afflicted, the widow and the orphan…

Never have we seen any Christian minister, of any degree or denomination, of his own church or of any other, in our times, fill so large a circle of the public mind. When we have walked with him in the crowded city, we have seen men's eyes greeting him as they passed. If we have travelled with him into the country, every church and every chapel in which he ministered was crowded to hear him…

And now we shall see his face no more; we shall hear his voice no more at our board; no longer shall we have his sympathies, and the aid of his energetic and benevolent spirit. We resolve unanimously that this committee shall now take measures to join their Christian brethren of all denominations to do him honour at his grave.

Rowland was buried, at his own request, in a brick vault beneath the pulpit of Surrey Chapel, on Friday 19 April 1833. Before the funeral a large number of ministers met at the chapel house and the aged Dr Rippon prayed 'for the sanctification of the event to all connected with the departed minister'. Soon after eleven the body was taken from the house into the chapel, with Collyer of Peckham and Thomas Jackson leading the way. Rowland's nephew, Lord Hill, the commander in chief of the British forces, along with his aide de camp Captain George Hill, attended as chief mourners. Clergymen and dissenting ministers of various denominations sustained the pall, and they were followed by the trustees of the chapel, the executors, the private friends of Rowland, the ministers who had long supplied his pulpit, the deputations from several religious societies and the servants of the family. One of the ministers was Theophilus Jones, Rowland's Wotton assistant, who went to the funeral while suffering from pneumonia. The journey to London, and the sorrows of losing such a dear friend, aggravated his condition to such an extent that he died a few weeks later.

The huge congregation began to assemble at nine o'clock and to avoid confusion they were admitted by ticket only. By ten o'clock every seat was filled in the chapel, except for those reserved for the mourners and close friends. The pulpit, desks and the whole front gallery were covered in black cloth. The women from the alms-houses appeared in the clothes Rowland had provided for them and the children of the School of Industry were suitably attired in emblems of mourning. Many shops shut during the service, private houses closed their blinds, and the crowds all dressed in black who could not gain admittance to the ceremony, showed by their sorrow the respect in which he was held.

As Rowland's body entered the chapel a dirge was played on the organ. The coffin was placed before the pulpit, over the vault that had been prepared for it. Collyer and Jackson read the burial service psalms alternately. The former also read 1 Corinthians 15 and then the first part of the actual service, which he did his best to abbreviate in accordance with the wish of William Jay, who had asked, 'How can I preach before persons who have been in the crowded chapel since nine o'clock in the morning?' At the request of Rowland's executors and the trustees of Surrey Chapel, Jackson read the rest of the funeral service. A hymn was sung.

The coffin was gently lowered into the grave amidst the weeping of the watching multitude. When the minister who read the conclusion of the service changed the word *brother* for that of *father* (a similar alteration had been made at the funeral of John Wesley), the grief of the congregation intensified to such a point that those who had so far restrained themselves burst forth in loud cryings. One poor woman, 'whose appearance did not bespeak attendance on the means of grace, said to her neighbour, "Well, he was a good man!"' George Clayton prayed and then the congregation sang Luther's hymn. William Jay, who for nearly fifty years had been one of the most acceptable preachers in the chapel and a great friend of Rowland's, then entered the pulpit to deliver the funeral sermon from Zechariah 11:2. 'There he lies,' said Jay pointing to the grave over which he was preaching. 'Who lies? The *preacher* once, the *witness* now.' Jay afterwards published his sermon under the title *Sensibility at the Fall of Eminence*.

George Collison of Hackney offered up the concluding prayer. Then the congregation filed slowly past the coffin, with one final look towards the man who had so influenced their lives. William Jones described the affecting scene:

There stood one of the heroes of Waterloo, with the star of his order glittering on his breast, looking at the last earthly home of a most endeared relative, whose prayers had often ascended to God on his behalf. There also was the aged clerk of the chapel, who for fifty years had been connected with its religious services. His head was supported upon his knee, the foot resting upon a hassock. His eye seemed immovably fixed on the tomb, and his tears witnessed how much he respected the departed. There the ministers of the gospel beheld the earthly house of their venerable father, and silently exclaimed, 'May we also be faithful unto death, and may our last end be like his.' The widow, the orphan, the Sabbath school teacher, the visitors of the poor and afflicted, and the aged tenants of the alms-houses raised by the deceased, all surrounded the grave. Earthly distinctions were forgotten, and amidst the sorrows of the scene, all rejoiced that their pastor was 'Not lost, but gone before'.

An old member of Surrey Chapel, in his recollections of Rowland, said,

As I beheld the ponderous coffin lowered into the tomb that had been built beneath the pulpit he had so long and faithfully occupied, I felt greatly oppressed, and inwardly cried, 'My father! My father!' for I had long loved him with a filial tenderness. A solemn procession was afterwards formed of the weeping congregation, which slowly moved round the open sepulchre, and as I took a last farewell of that which contained all that was left on earth of my beloved pastor, an aged fellow-labourer behind me whispered in my ear, 'Be not slothful, but followers of them who through faith and patience inherit the promises.'

There were several funeral sermons preached in Rowland's memory. Griffin, in his sermon, mentioned the time Rowland preached in a field at Portsea to a large congregation from the text, 'It is a faithful saying and worthy of all acceptation, that Christ Jesus came into the world to save sinners.' Four persons were afterwards admitted into church membership, who attributed their conversions to Rowland's sermon, and one of them became a deacon.

On Monday 22 April, the directors of the London Missionary Society met and expressed the loss that the society had sustained in Rowland's death. They called him 'one of the brightest ornaments of the age, in which he lived' and 'for more than threescore years one of the greatest blessings to the church'. They rejoiced that he was one of the founders of the society and one of the preachers who, 'at its first formation, publicly advocated its claims—that from its commencement the Society has received his entire approbation, his ardent attachment, his ready and effective service, and his liberal support; and the last public service for which he allowed himself to be announced, was to preside at a meeting of its friends'. They prayed 'that the mantle of the departed may descend on his survivors, and that the Lord may raise up others who shall emulate his labours'.

A marble tablet, surmounted by a bust of Rowland, was erected in Surrey Chapel on the front of the organ gallery, with the following inscription written by Sidney at the request of the trustees:

To the memory of the late
REVEREND ROWLAND HILL, A.M.
formerly of
Saint John's College, Cambridge,
and for
half a century the zealous, active and devoted
minister of Surrey Chapel;
this tablet is erected, rather in token
of
the grateful recollections of
a revered pastor,
by his bereaved and mourning congregation,
than as a tribute
suitable to the worth of one
the
imperishable monuments of whose labours
are the
names written in heaven of the multitudes
led to God by his long and
faithful ministry.

To this inscription the trustees simply added the dates of his birth, death and interment.

20. The character of the man

Rowland was above average height and when young was very thin, though strong and active. His countenance was expressive and the piercing look that came from his small grey eyes denoted both intelligence and humour. When between fifty and sixty his figure was upright, 'with a high bred, gentleman like deportment', and twenty five years later his form was not bowed down or the vigour of his mind in the slightest degree impaired. Once a man in a country town followed a crowd into a chapel without knowing the name of the preacher. He returned home and said, 'I have seen a man with *such a commanding air* as I never witnessed before—who can it be?' The man was Rowland Hill. A life of temperance and exertion meant that he enjoyed a high degree of health and was rarely curtailed in his activities through sickness.

William Jay, who knew Rowland for forty-seven years and who preached annually at Surrey Chapel for forty-six years, enjoyed free access to him in private and had many opportunities to judge his character in public. He said that 'never was there a man more open to observation, and never was there a man more qualified to bear it; for he had all the transparency of glass without the brittleness'. Jay said of Rowland that 'he passed through life with unblemished reputation, and left a character without a single stain', and 'he was from the beginning a peculiar individual, a perfectly original character'.

One of Rowland's frequent sayings was, 'What is a minister without a *character*?' It was his aim in life at all times to be holy. George Weight said that 'it was the holiness of his mind which originated his fervent and entire devotion to the cause of Christ; *this* was the source of all his mighty efforts for the temporal and eternal welfare of mankind; *this* was the master spring which animated the whole machine of his extensive benevolence'. Once he was called upon to occupy the pulpit of a man of dubious character, who apologized because he could not offer him a cassock. 'Sir,' replied Rowland, who could not hide his feelings, 'I can preach without my *cassock*, but not without my *character*—character is of immense importance, sir, to a preacher of God's holy gospel.' Personal holiness was the striking feature of his life.

Rowland always encouraged young ministers to live a consistent and blameless life, if they desired to be an effective preacher of the gospel. Once, when addressing candidates for the sacred office at one of the London dissenting colleges and in order to make his point, he told this story:

A barber having amassed a comfortable independence, retired to his native place, where he became a preacher in a small chapel. Another person from the same village, being similarly fortunate, settled there also, and attended the ministry of the barber. Wanting a new wig, he said to his pastor, '*You* might as well make it for me,' to which he assented. The wig was sent home badly made, but charged at nearly double the usual price! The good man said nothing, but when anything particularly profitable escaped the lips of the preacher, he observed to himself, 'Excellent!—but *oh! the wig!*' When the barber prayed with apparent unction, he also thought, 'This should touch my heart—but *oh! the wig!*' Now my dear young brethren, wherever you are placed, *remember the wig!*'

He was also keen to impress on the minds of young ministers the importance of letting 'their moderation be known unto all men' in their daily conversations with people, a practice he was careful to follow at his own table. He was a remarkably small eater and rarely allowed himself more than two glasses of wine after his dinner. He was particularly careful to adhere to this rule when he was travelling, for he had often witnessed the evils that accompany indiscretion in this area. Not only that, but he discovered from years of observing people and society that, generally speaking, the persons who encouraged ministers to indulge in the 'good things of the world', were the first to expose them to public disgrace if they went beyond the bounds of moderation.

Rowland was a deeply humble man, who was often 'humbled in the dust' on hearing of the success of his preaching, and would exclaim with feeling, 'Lord, I am an unprofitable servant.' In humility he remarked that while the minds of many old men seemed to him like ample storehouses, filled with a rich variety of materials, he could compare his own to a closet, containing a few good thoughts, to be produced as occasion required. Edwin Sidney comments that 'although the love of approbation was the leading quality of his mind, he never once forgot, in the midst of the applause which welcomed him everywhere in his latter days, to prostrate himself in the dust and ashes before God, and the riper he became in grace, the more fervent were his supplications for humility'. When he drew near to his Father in prayer he felt 'a worm, and no man'.

In his public and private life, Rowland enjoyed an intimacy with God, with the spirit of prayer continually resting on his mind. He consecrated all his talents at the throne of grace and maintained his spiritual fervour through prayer. In fact, he was so familiar with prayer that there were only a few intervals during the day when his heart was not drawn up to God. He once said, 'I like ejaculatory prayer: it reaches heaven before the devil can get a shot at it.' His friends were not in his presence for long without hearing him pray. He spent a great deal of time in secret prayer, although he was fairly brief in family devotions.

Robert Dabney, in his *Systematic Theology*, wrote, 'Prayer is not intended to produce a change in God, but in us,' and then went on to quote Rowland: 'Rowland Hill explained to sailors, "The man in the skiff at the stern of a man-of-war, does not pull the ship to himself, in hauling at the line, but pulls the skiff to the ship. This line is prayer. Prayer does not draw God down to us, but draws us up to God, and thus establishes the connection."'

Rowland's generosity was 'unbounded'. Although the trustees of the chapel contributed towards the household charges at Surrey Chapel, Rowland's expenditure was far greater than this allowance. However, he was sufficiently well off not to need a regular salary for his services. He had no love of money and only valued it as a means of doing good.

Rowland Hill's almshouses

Such was the generosity of his nature that he would have given away all he possessed if it had not been for the restraining influence of his wife. The chapel house was often crowded with the needy, and rarely did a genuine sufferer apply to him in vain. However, he strongly opposed the idea adopted by many ministers of selling their own publications, which he regarded as a 'genteel mode of begging'.

During William Jones's last conversation with Rowland, the aged patriarch gave him a donation for a poor minister, while intimating to his friend that he gave approximately two thirds of his annual income to charitable purposes, thus fulfilling his own advice, 'Such as have it in their power should make *the poor man's pocket the bank of their riches.*' As can be imagined, he did not hesitate to condemn the mean. 'A miser,' he said, 'is like a pig, of no use until he is dead and cut up.' 'There are some persons,' he remarked on another occasion, 'who are so little regretted when they die, that the last thing you hear about them is, the payment of the undertaker's bill.'

There are numerous examples of his generosity and willingness to help others. Charles Spurgeon in his book *Eccentric Preachers* quotes Grant's sketch of Rowland found in *The Metropolitan Pulpit*. A pious woman, who was a member of Surrey Chapel, was married to an ungodly man, who spent his time drinking beer while she was at church. The couple fell into

Charles Spurgeon

financial difficulties and were unable to pay their rent, the consequence of which was that their furniture was confiscated. After despairing about what to do, the wife decided to approach Rowland. She went to his house and explained to him their situation.

'How much would you require to save your furniture and get rid of the person in possession?' enquired Mr Hill.

'Eighteen pounds, sir, would be quite sufficient for the purpose,' answered the poor woman, with a palpitating heart.

'I'll let you have the loan of twenty, and you can repay me at your convenience. Send your husband to me on your return, and I will have two ten pound notes ready by the time he arrives. I wish to give the notes to him rather than to you.'

Mrs D—quitted Mr Hill's house and hurried home with light foot, but with a still lighter heart. Having communicated to her husband what had passed between herself and her minister, it is unnecessary to say that he lost no time in proceeding to the house of Mr Hill. The latter received him with much kindness of manner.

'And so,' said he, 'you are so unfortunate as to have a person in possession.'

'We unfortunately have, sir.'

'And twenty pounds will be sufficient to get rid of him and restore your furniture to you?'

'It will, sir.'

'Well, then,' said Mr Hill, pointing to the table, 'there are two ten pound notes for you, which you can repay when you are able. Take them.'

'The other advanced to the table, took the notes, and was in the act of folding them up, at the same time warmly thanking Mr Hill for the act of friendship he had done him, and expressing a hope that he would soon be able to pay the amount back again, when the reverend gentleman suddenly exclaimed, 'Stop a little! Just lay the notes down again until I ask a blessing on them.'

The other did as he was desired, on which Mr Hill, extending both his arms uttered a short prayer to this effect:—'O Lord, who art the Author of all mercy and the Giver of every good and perfect gift, do thou be graciously pleased to bless the sum of money which is given to him who is now before thee, that it may conduce to his present and eternal welfare. For Jesus Christ's sake. Now, sir,' said Rowland Hill, as he finished his brief supplication, 'now, sir, you may take the money.'

The party a second time took up the two ten pound notes, and was in the act as before of folding them up, when Mr Hill interposed, by reminding him that he had forgotten one thing. It may be easily supposed that by this time he was a good deal confused. His confusion was increased a hundredfold when Mr Hill remarked, 'But, my friend, you have not yourself asked for a blessing on the money. You had better do it now.'

'Sir,' faltered out the other, scarcely able to support himself, 'sir, I cannot pray. I never prayed in all my life.'

'You have the more need to begin now,' observed the reverend gentleman, in his own cool yet rebuking manner.

'I cannot, sir; I do not know what to say.'

'Try, try and thank God and ask his blessing, however short your prayer may be.'

'I cannot, sir; I cannot say a single sentence.'

'Then you can't have the money. I will not lend twenty pounds to a prayerless man.'

The other hesitated for a moment, and then with closed eyes, and uplifted hands, he said with great earnestness, 'O Lord, what shall I say to thee and to Mr Hill on this occasion?'

He was about to begin another sentence, when the reverend gentleman interrupted him by observing, 'That will do for a beginning. It is a very excellent first prayer, for it is from the heart. Take the money, and may God's blessing be given along with it.' As he spoke, Mr Hill took up the two ten pound notes, and transferring them to the half-bewildered man, cordially shook him by the hand, and wished him good morning.

It only remains for me to mention, that not only did the husband and wife become prosperous in secular matters, but the incident made so deep an impression on the husband's mind as to end in his conversion to God.

In general conversation Rowland was particularly gifted. He had an 'uncommon quickness of apprehension, which will account for the great fund of general knowledge which he possessed; though he never seemed to study anything, or to read any book attentively through,—yet there was no subject upon which he seemed unable to speak; though in discourse he could never be kept long to any one point'. He was adept at finding an apt and striking illustration to make his point. Jay mentions one example in his biography of Cornelius Winter: 'His dear and honoured friend, Mr Hill, with his usual force and humour, said, "Mr Winter would make the worst devil of any man in the world,"' which was a singular way of showing his view of the meekness, gentleness and loveliness of his character.

Rowland's wit was one of the reasons why many came to hear him, and he had to be careful not to overuse it or to use it in an irreverent manner. Abner W. Brown said that 'there are some preachers whose nature seems to be a joke. Rowland Hill is one: joking seems to be the mould he is cast in; he is a good man, and I believe he cannot help joking, and therefore I hope God accepts him in it'. In some senses Brown was right. During an evening service, for instance, a heavy shower caused several persons to take shelter in Surrey Chapel while he was preaching. Seeing the crowd by the gallery doors, and never being one to miss an opportunity, he remarked, 'Many people are greatly to be blamed for making their religion a *cloak*, but I do not think those are much better who make it an *umbrella*.'

Rowland uncovered his heart when he said, 'I never desire to laugh one moment if I cannot pray the next,' and on this principle he uniformly acted; 'for though in his conversation, and sometimes in his sermons, you saw the sparklings of his wit, and smiled at the drollery of his allusions; yet through all this you perceived that he was the man of God, that he was aiming at the benefit of your souls, and that he sought not your applause, but your salvation'.

Rowland's wit and humour occasionally gave offence and caused him to be spoken against. Sometimes he used it to good effect when giving a word of rebuke. A conceited young man called on him one day when he was at William Jay's house, and asked him if he had heard that he was going to change his sentiments. 'No, sir,' replied Rowland, 'I have not; but, if you have not fixed the time, I would advise you to do it as near the change of the moon as possible.' On another occasion a talkative woman said to him, 'I have been a good deal of late with some papists, and they have sadly tempted me to change my religion.' 'Indeed, ma'am,' he replied, 'I was not aware until now that you had any religion to change.'

Once he visited with Mrs Hill the house of a clerical friend, when the host and his wife started insensitively reviewing the characters of many of their personal friends and acquaintances. Rowland said nothing but became increasingly irritated by the conversation. To put an end to it he stood up and rang the bell. When the servant appeared he asked for a hearth brush and dustpan, and when they arrived he began to sweep the carpet, 'saying that a prodigious quantity of dust and dirt had been scattered that evening by his two companions, and he was anxious to have it removed!' The hint was taken and the conversation turned onto another subject.

Spurgeon, while admitting that Rowland had a humorous streak, rightly said that he was 'a great deal more' and should not be remembered simply for his humour in the pulpit.

Those who know his life-work [remarked Spurgeon] will not remember him as exemplifying one single quality, but as a great, good, child-like man in whom nothing was repressed, but the whole of his redeemed nature allowed to have harmonious play. Take him for all in all, we shall not soon look upon his like again. In him was no guile. He loved his Lord and the souls of men, and he threw all his might into the pursuit of doing good. Surely no man was ever more unselfish, or less self-conscious. Men called him eccentric because they themselves were out of centre; he with his great heart, calm soul, wise mind, and loving nature had learned to wait upon the Lord, and so had found the right centre and true orbit for his being. At first the press had its sneers for him, but it could not lessen the respect in which he was held, and in due time it turned round and joined in the chorus of his praise. His riper years were full of honour, and, like his younger days, full of fruit unto God.

Rowland possessed a deep and natural affection for the members of his family. In the words of Sidney, 'It was impossible to be the inmate of his house and not love him; he neglected none of those little acts of kindness, which make up the sum of human happiness in private life; and his uniform cheerfulness gave an inexpressible charm to the circle of his fireside.' He also acted in a true Christian manner towards his servants and he felt keenly for their temporal and spiritual welfare.

Rowland was so absent minded that he desperately needed his servant's constant attention. Before he went to chapel Charles would often go through a 'check list' to make sure he had everything he needed. 'Have you got your spectacles, sir?' 'Yes, Charles.' 'Your white pocket handkerchief?' 'Yes, Charles.' 'Your coloured one?' 'Yes, Charles.' Even then it was necessary to keep a sharp look out or he would leave without his hat. William Jones ate breakfast with him during Mrs Hill's illness and noticed that he took the egg boiler from the fire and replaced it again, but without the egg. He then put water in the teapot, but forgot to put in the tea. When he poured it out, he observed, 'It is very weak and must stand a little longer.' He then remembered the egg and cried, 'Oh, my egg, it will be overdone.' He tried to find the egg but in vain, and smiled when he realised what he had done. 'Are you sure, sir, that you put tea into your teapot,' enquired Jones. He looked into the pot and found there was none, and laughed heartily at his mistake.

As with all men, Rowland had his weaknesses. According to Jackson of Stockwell he was

...naturally haughty; his firmness sometimes degenerated into obstinacy; he found it difficult to forgive an injury; he was sometimes hasty and indiscriminate in his attachments, which occasionally involved him in difficulties: but he was deeply sensible of his defects; and if at any time he had been overtaken in a fault, the writer has been affected to see him weeping bitterly, and in the most humiliating terms, imploring forgiveness through a Saviour's blood.

One of his failings was his willingness to listen to flatterers, who would then influence him with their critical remarks about others. At Surrey Chapel there were a few members who always expressed their deep regret at his absence and told him that no supply preached with his power and authority. Once they had gained his attention, they made unkind comments about certain individuals—comments that Rowland was all too ready to believe. If they knew Rowland had an unfavourable opinion of a particular minister, they would collect all the gossip about him and prejudice their pastor's mind, who in turn appeared to possess an unforgiving spirit.

William Jay reckoned that his greatest weakness was an

…extremely quick sense of any injury or offence, and allowing it to *linger* about his spirit. The offence, too, was sometimes supposed, rather than real; or credited on the evidence of some tattler, or busybody, who too often beset him, and was not sufficiently frowned off. His high regard for moral consistency would be enough to make one impropriety or indiscretion undo much of an opposite quality; and where there was anything actually peccable in the character of a professor, or especially of a minister, the spirituality and purity of his mind would render it more intolerable to him than it would be to many men.

Jay also disagreed with some who thought candour was one of Rowland's greatest qualities. 'Among his own immediate connexions, he expected implicit submission, and his will was law. Of other parties, who differed from him, he could speak freely. He did not always distinguish between bigotry and regularity, nor consider that persons were not to be run down as illiberal, because they acted conscientiously and did not feel themselves at liberty to tread in all his steps.' He was not very candid or courteous towards Baptists, and would sometimes insult them when he administered the ordinance of infant baptism.

Sometimes he was not only unkind in the things he said about others, but became too personal in his attacks on them. He tended to express his views in such away that they could be misinterpreted. Jamieson was not far from the truth when he called Rowland 'a bigot for liberality'. Once he was talking with an Independent minister, when he remarked with great feeling, 'I *hate in*dependency.' 'Yes, sir,' was the reply, 'and you hate *de*pendency just as much,' which again was very close to the mark.

As he mellowed in later years, he mourned over some of the things he had said, and the past bitterness in controversy was deeply regretted by him. In his own walk with God he practised daily penitence and was fond of repeating the idea that 'if I may be permitted to drop one tear, as I enter the portals of the city of my God, it will be at taking an eternal leave of that beloved and profitable companion, *Repentance*'. He also received letters of apology from persons who had spoken unkindly about him.

His choice of friends was not always wise and he 'received more than once a scorpion into his bosom'. One incident of this kind led him to appear in an unfavourable light to several respected clergymen. His opinion of a man's character was not always accurate, which caused him to place unguarded confidence in unworthy individuals. He occasionally praised his friends too highly, so that what he said bordered on the extravagant and fanciful. He said of one minister, who preached at the Tabernacle at Wotton, 'If we had a dozen such preachers as—in the land, we should soon drive the devil out of it.' He also expected his friends to follow his lead, saying of a minister whom he had been the means of leading to God, and who possessed an independent mind, 'He is a nice lad, but he will have his own way.'

21. A true shepherd

Rowland's incessant preaching engagements and the number of members in his church, which at one time amounted to nearly 800, made it difficult for him to carry out his pastoral duties efficiently, but he was always on the lookout for ways to strengthen his people's faith.

He was careful not to visit his people too often, in case they came to resent his presence, or to visit them too sporadically and so feel neglected. He regularly talked to the women in the alms-houses and was at times frustrated by their lack of Christian contentment. He strongly urged the poor to adorn the Christian character, particularly with cleanliness, and was certain that a slovenly person and a dirty house were evidence that there had been no change of heart. He frequently remarked, '*I don't know how godliness and filthiness can dwell together.*' Once he went to a cottage where, among other symptoms of uncleanness, he noticed some dirty rabbits in the corner of a room. As soon as he saw them he said to the woman in a quite unique way, 'Mistress, I suppose you put those creatures there that one nasty smell may drive out another.'

George Clayton found nothing in life that he looked back upon with more pleasure than the 'neighbourly and friendly' conversations he enjoyed for many years with Rowland. One morning he called on him at Surrey Chapel house. Rowland, who was then more than eighty years old, immediately invited him to join him on his pastoral visits.

He first conducted me to the alms-houses, and passing from one apartment to another, he gave a word of exhortation and comfort to the old ladies; and with one of them, confined by illness, he offered up a prayer, very short, but admirable for its simplicity, spirituality and adaptation. We then proceeded to some of the most wretched hovels, which abound in the back streets of that neighbourhood. Several of these were inhabited by pious poor. He spoke to them with tender sympathy, and the most lovely condescension. One or two he admonished for their slovenly neglect and want of cleanliness, reminding them that godliness should make people tidy and clean in their habits. With some he left money; with some he offered prayer—to all he gave kind looks, kind words and his blessing. Coming out of a room that was certainly *very dirty*, he exclaimed, 'We must endure all things for the salvation of souls.'

After this, we entered the habitation of others of his charge, moving in what is called a respectable sphere of life. Among these, some of whom were the principal trades people in Southwark, he dropped a word in season, comforting the afflicted, warning their minds against impatience and fretfulness, and exhorting to perseverance and prayer. It was truly edifying to observe how he changed his tone and manner, according to the requirements of the case, and how truly 'grace was poured into his lips' while he went from house to house, as 'the shepherd of his people'.

The above is an accurate description of Rowland's mode of visiting his hearers and his kindness towards them often made them more receptive to his sermons.

He was ever faithful to the truth when he spoke to the dying, and his concluding prayer rarely failed to touch their hearts. His attitude and feelings towards his dying friends are well expressed by Sidney:

His calmness in the chamber of the dying, the tenderness with which he held forth the love of Jesus, as the only refuge of the expiring believer, and his composed and solemn commendation of the soul to God, were wonderfully contrasted with his agitation, when he left the bedside of one he loved, but whom he was soon to lose. The emotions he had suppressed, often vented themselves on these occasions in tears, but oftener in a violent sickness, which would have alarmed a stranger, and was most distressing to his friends. Nor did his anxiety for his dying hearers end with the ebullition of his sorrow; he thought of them often and sometimes composed hymns, which he sent them.

There were times when Rowland, as a preacher, found it difficult to empathise fully with the poor and needy in his congregation, partly because his own path had been 'even and pleasant' and he had not endured similar sufferings. His sermons, therefore, did not contain many experimental observations.

Rowland exhorted parents to be a holy example to their children. Once, when referring to the bad behaviour of children whose parents professed to be Christians, he remarked, 'Through a long life I have invariably noticed, that when such children turn out improperly, you may trace a defect in the religious character of one, or both, of the parents. If the father is a godly man, the wife may have much of the world about her; or, if the mother is wholly devoted to God, the children may see a want of cooperation in the father in advancing the mother's plans.' He urged parents to punish their children 'as the Lord corrects his, never in wrath, but always in mercy. Every stripe given by an angry hand, from a revengeful heart, only increases the evil for which the child is so unwisely and unworthily corrected.' He thought a volatile disposition in a child needed 'regulation [rather] than reproof'. Parents must be loved 'before they can be obeyed, unless by terror, which only excites the obedience of vile servility, and which consequently creates detestation; when from the fear of these things the mind is emancipated, the worst of consequences must ensue from such an ill-judged education'.

Many people called on Rowland each week with various problems and requests. Some wanted his advice about working for the government or entering the army, others wanted his views on their suitability for the ministry, while others asked for food or money. With gentleness and wisdom, based on many years of experience, he dealt with each matter as it arose.

One man, who had been converted under one of Rowland's sermons soon after the erection of Surrey Chapel, became blind and rather senile in his old age, and wanted to become the 'poet laureate of the Evangelical Magazine'. Every month he sent Rowland his dictated poems and asked him to insert them in the magazine. Rowland, not wanting to offend his old friend, used to take down a volume of the magazine and place the poems in it, and then tell the messenger who had brought them, 'Give my love to Mr—, and say I have put his verses into the magazine.' He felt it was better to please him in this way than to upset him needlessly in the time of his decline.

As a pastor he was unafraid of rebuking others and was grieved at the failings of Christians and particularly of Christian ministers, whom he watched over with jealousy, and was adept at making the most of opportunities to rebuke blameworthy habits in his hearers. One of his hearers who, much to his annoyance, did not come to chapel for the prayers, but turned up just in time for the sermon, complained to him of 'partiality in a magistrate'. Rowland gave him a searching look and then growled out, 'Then, why do you not come to public prayers in proper time to pray that God would "grant all magistrates grace to execute justice and maintain truth"?'

A member of his congregation was in the habit of going to the theatre, so Rowland challenged him by saying,

'This will never do—a member of my church in the habit of attending the theatre!'

'There must be some mistake,' responded the startled man. 'I am not in the habit of going there, although I admit I go now and then *for a treat.*'

'Oh,' said Rowland, 'then you are a worse hypocrite than ever, sir. Suppose anyone spread the report that I ate carrion, and I answered, "Well, there is no wrong in that; I don't eat carrion every day in the week, but I have a dish now and then *for a treat!*" Why, you would say, "What a nasty, foul, and filthy appetite Rowland Hill has, to have to go to carrion for a treat." Religion is the Christian's truest treat, Christ is his enjoyment.'

Once he heard that a preacher, who spoke eloquently in the pulpit, was treating his wife unkindly, so he determined to make a morning call on him, and he took a young unmarried minister with him in his carriage. When he arrived at the minister's door, he apologized to the servant for not getting out of the carriage, on account of his increasing weakness. The minister and his wife soon came to the door and Rowland spoke to the latter in a most respectful way, while virtually ignoring her husband. All his conversation was directed her way until he mentioned to his young companion how he ought to treat his wife, if he was ever blessed with such a helpmate. His remarks were delivered in a 'soft, subdued tone, but they produced the desired effect on the silent husband'.

On one occasion he was preaching for the Missionary Society and was accompanied to the chapel by several ministers and other Christian friends. After the service he returned home by boat and soon discovered that one of the party, who was acting foolishly, had had too much to drink. Turning to his servant he said in a loud voice, 'Charles, when you see a parson drunk, don't talk about it, for you will injure the cause of religion; but whenever you see me drunk, tell the world about it.'

Rowland made the most of every opportunity in his correspondence to encourage and advise others. He was quite prepared to correspond with children and, in a letter to the little daughter of his friend Wathen, he not only made her smile with his gentle humour, but passed on practical advice for her to follow:

MY DEAR MISS WATHEN,

How kind to correspond with such an old man, old enough to be your great grandfather. Should I ever be ground young again, I shall certainly remember your kind attention to me; but as I cannot find out where the mill is to be found that grinds old people into young ones, I can only advise my young friend, Miss Wathen, to follow the excellent advice of her parents, whereby she will be directed to be wise and good; but not without the Lord should bless her with his grace, whereby she alone can be enabled to live to his glory. With love to your most dear parents, believe me to be,

Most affectionately yours,

ROWLAND HILL.

Rowland always strove to help those who were persecuted for their faith at home or who experienced religious conflicts with members of their family. To one young woman, who had been told by her parents not to talk about religion, and who was wondering if she should obey their injunction, Rowland advised her to use 'no other weapons but those of sound arguments' and 'by the most persuasive mildness to win by love, as well as to convince by truth'. In this way, he hoped the parents would 'feel their mistake, and find it their duty to permit you to live comfortably at home, and allow at least some variation of sentiments in you, which may not be altogether conformable to their own... If you can give good advice to such as are bad, and direct them to the Saviour that he may change their hearts, I must say that no parental authority should prevent you from so good a work.'

These brief extracts show Rowland to be a true shepherd of the flock under his care, and a pastor who was vigilant, affectionate, patient and wise in his dealings with others.

22. The preacher

When Rowland was still a youth, he was once preaching by his father's park at Hawkstone. His voice was sufficiently strong at times to carry to Sir Rowland, who was sitting in his drawing room, confined by the gout. Sir Rowland, displeased with his sons for preaching in villages and fields, sent a servant to fetch Richard. When Richard arrived, he asked him whose voice he could hear. 'It is Rowland, I suppose, Sir, preaching to the people in the neighbourhood.' Sir Rowland ordered Richard to tell his brother to come to him immediately. Richard obeyed and whispered to Rowland that he must go directly to his father. Rowland replied, 'What shall I do with the congregation? I cannot go unless you come up and finish my discourse.' Richard immediately began to preach while Rowland went to his father, who lectured him on his irregular conduct.

During the lecture, Sir Rowland inquired, 'I hear some other person preaching now—who is that?' 'I suppose it is Richard, finishing my sermon, Sir,' answered Rowland. 'Go immediately,' retorted his father, 'and tell him I command him to come at once to me, and do you come with him.' Rowland went straightaway, but when he arrived, Richard had finished preaching and the people had been dismissed. They both went to their father, who severely scolded them for 'degrading themselves'. The brothers answered respectfully and related some humorous anecdotes about the thankful expressions of the poor elderly women, which made their father, in spite of his anger, smile, for he was pleased that the people in the neighbourhood should be kept in good humour. After Sir Rowland's anger had died down, the two brothers bowed and retired.

Throughout his life Rowland was never entirely happy with his own preaching, and on many occasions he declared that he 'never reached the foot of the pulpit stairs without the impression that he had not discharged his office as he ought'. When he dwelt on the great truths of the gospel, he would interject, 'But I cannot reach those lofty themes with the poor little pigmy powers of *my* mind.' Occasionally he said, 'When I am in the pulpit I think no one preaches so badly; but when I am out of it, listening to others, then I think no one preaches so well.' When he heard men such as Chalmers, Robert Hall, William Jay and others, he cried, 'I can never preach again.'

He was often anxious about the solemn work of preaching. At times, before he entered the pulpit, he seemed lost in reflection and would occasionally whisper, 'Lord, help me to preach.' On one occasion, a colonel in the engineers, to whom his ministry had been blessed, was keen to be introduced to him. In the evening of the day on which they met, Rowland was to preach in Woolwich, and he asked his new friend to join him in his carriage. A dog also jumped into the carriage and made itself at home. The officer hoped for some godly conversation as they rode along, but Rowland appeared unconscious of his presence, and started to whisper to himself about the arrangement of his sermon, while pulling at the hairs on the dog's back and spreading them on the colonel's knee! The colonel was very amused at the great preacher's 'absence', and was pleased his train of thought was not interrupted, 'for such a sermon as Mr Hill preached that night he had never heard before'.

According to some observant members of his congregations, it was possible to predict what kind of sermon he was about to deliver by the way he climbed the pulpit stairs. If he seemed anxious to seat people in empty pews and was busy with unimportant matters, it was an indication that the sermon was likely to be 'of the rambling order'; but if he climbed the stairs 'abstracted from every surrounding circumstance', pausing now and then as if in prayer, it was likely to be a 'profitable season'. His prayer would be short and his sermon full of the truth as it is in Jesus.

Rowland's sermons have been described as 'expository lectures', although sometimes, when he enlarged on the context, he did not reach his text before it was time to conclude. In this he followed his own advice to preachers, 'to take plenty of elbow room'. Once a member of his congregation said to him, 'Mr Hill, you have taken us from Dan to Beersheba in your sermon today.' 'Never mind, my friend,' he gentle responded, 'it's all holy ground.' His brother Richard once complained about Rowland's 'elbow room': 'When a man gives out a text, he raises my expectation to hear *that* text explained and improved; and I feel disappointed, though I hear as good, or better things, from any other words.'

The *Cabinet Annual Register* for 1833 gave an accurate picture of Rowland's preaching:

As a preacher, Mr Hill was extremely unequal, as well as systematically unmethodical; generally rambling, but pithy, often throwing out the most striking remarks, and sometimes interspersing touches of genuine pathos, amid much that bordered upon the ludicrous. But even in his most grotesque sallies, there was a redeeming simplicity of purpose and seriousness of intention. You felt that the preacher did not mean to trifle; that there was no attempt at display, no unhallowed familiarity in his feelings, or want of reverence to sacred things. In his more private expository exercises, he was generally grave and edifying, with few inequalities, and often highly impressive.

He was first and foremost an extemporaneous preacher. William Jay remarked that he 'spoke almost perfectly extemporaneously', but was 'not always guarded in his imagery and diction'. Rowland strongly opposed ministers reading their sermons.

The dull modern way of reading, instead of preaching, from the pulpit, I rather choose to leave to others, than to practise myself, as it only tends to lull people to sleep, and to cast additional loads of ignorance upon our ministers. If a minister, after having duly considered the leading truths of his text, would but venture, under the divine blessing, to enforce the subject from the natural ability which God may have given him, he would find his heart animated by the subject, and preaching would soon be his *daily* delight.

Apart from the occasional 'failure', preaching was certainly Rowland's *daily* delight. He once said, 'Such delight do I feel in my work, that I could almost wish there might be preaching in heaven.' Sidney said, 'Never were the faculties of any human being more completely devoted to one object, than his were to the exercise of his ministry, and the motives which animated his exertions were as pure as they were powerful.' When travelling for the cause of the gospel Rowland occasionally preached more than twenty sermons in a week. 'I do not think,' he said humorously, 'that once in my life I did earn my daily bread. I was spending several weeks with a friend in North Wales, and she made me preach for every meal, so that before breakfast, dinner, tea and supper, I had to ascend the pulpit.'

On one occasion, when he was with a minister who had retired from active service, and only occasionally preached, he remarked, 'I would sooner wear out, than rust out.' A couple of his favourite comments were: 'If some ministers were to be fed according to their preaching, they would not look so plump as they do.' 'Of all the diseases a man can die of, to die of fat and laziness is the worst.'

Until near the time of his death, Rowland preached twice on Sundays, addressed the members of his church on Monday evenings, and preached lectures in his chapel on Tuesday evenings and Friday mornings, in addition to taking other services. When he was ill and unable to preach, a close watch was usually kept over him, as there was a danger that as soon as he heard the distant notes of the organ, he would get up and go to the chapel. Once he was confined because of inflamed eyes, which were covered with protecting bandages. Just as the people approached the Lord's Table, he made his appearance. He wore a large blue cloak, and although blindfolded had found his way from the house to the chapel without any help. His sudden entrance visibly excited the congregation, and as the officiating ministers were urging him to retire, he exclaimed, 'My dear people, they won't let me say one word to you!' He then pronounced a brief but touching benediction on them and left the chapel.

Rowland thought one of the best ways to fight off illness was to preach. He often said 'a good pulpit perspiration is a famous thing to keep a man in good health'. Once, when Rowland met Dr Waugh at the recognition service of John Arundel as the pastor of a church in the borough of Southwark, he responded to some remarks that had been made about his 'good old age', by saying, 'I dare say you young ministers would be glad to live to be old men. Now, I will tell you how to obtain your wishes—preach three times a day, and seven days in the week, and then you'll find not only that you are in a fine state of health, but that you stand a good chance of becoming old men.'

Chapter 22

W. Richards summed up Rowland's immense amount of labour by saying,

Sixty-six years did he labour in his Lord's vineyard, a term seldom paralleled in modern times; and when we take into account the frequency of his preaching, the extraordinary exertions which were required of him in order to make himself heard by the thousands always, and tens of thousands at times, who followed him; one is astonished to think how his clay tenement was sustained under it. Not only did he labour, during the greater part of his life, more abundantly than almost any of his contemporaries, but his bodily exertions far exceeded those of any other preacher since Mr Whitefield's death.

Rowland had a commanding and dignified presence in the pulpit, a unique mode of address and a natural eloquence, which his printed sermons fail to portray. His voice was full, clear and melodious, and he could be clearly heard by the largest congregations in the open air, even towards the end of his life. He was not a 'mere boisterous bawler', as some who had never heard him reported. 'He was sometimes loud, and occasionally even vehement; but in common his voice only rose with his subject; and it was easy to perceive that it was commonly influenced and regulated by his thoughts and feelings.' Sometimes he brought in anecdotes too abruptly, mainly because he had run out of subject matter. He possessed a good command of language, sometimes using his vocabulary to striking effect. Simplicity and deep feeling characterized his sermons, and he addressed people as one who felt the importance of his office.

His sentences were free, detached and striking, and he seldom spoke without uttering something sublime and pathetic. So important were his one-off sentences that from the year 1800 to his last sermon many were taken down, 'with strict accuracy and correctness, as they fell from the lips of that dear faithful minister of Christ', by William Collyer, who published them under the title *Pulpit Sayings* in 1835.

Sidney called his preaching an 'uninterrupted stream of ideas from a warm heart and fertile imagination, mingled with every species of similitude that suggested itself to his mind at the moment'. Robert Hall, himself an accomplished preacher, who had heard men of the calibre and brilliance of Christmas Evans, said of him, 'No man has ever drawn, since the days of our Saviour, such sublime images from nature; here Mr Hill excels every other man.' Sometimes he described so vividly the scenes of eternal glory, that the hearers were convinced he had already seen them for himself and was reporting back to them.

Rowland's sudden outpourings of eloquence were more dramatic for being unrehearsed as an idea came to him as he was speaking, often with reference to some present object. 'He was remarkable,' said one, 'for occasionally seizing a powerful thought, darting it into the soul like lightning, where it would hold as though fastened by a nail. He had the passions of his audience at command.' Another witness said that his 'voice would rise into one of those bursts of impassioned declamation, on the purity of God, which often made the very hair tingle, and the place to appear as holy ground'. 'Like those of Whitefield, the bursts were occasional, and excited by the energy of feeling at the moment. There was nothing he so much disliked as a tame smoothness of language that slid off from the mind and conscience of the hearer.'

He had a singular facility of communicating with the uneducated, without talking down to them, but rather, by simple illustrations, gently bringing them up to a higher level of understanding. In a letter signed by 'A Christian', the writer said that the mode of Rowland's preaching was 'purposely adapted to the cases and capacities of the poorer sort. After the manner of our blessed Saviour's parables, his illustrations are plain, simple, and drawn from nature; and ... often interspersed with striking anecdotes and examples suited to the subject he is upon.'

Once Rowland travelled on behalf of the London Missionary Society to an agricultural district, where he had a congregation of farmers and their labourers, who were not used to thinking deeply. He wanted to answer the questions: 'Have not the heathen sufficient light? And if so, why should we trouble ourselves about them?' He first admitted the fact before saying that they did not use the light they had properly. He then used the following illustration:

He supposed the whole family at the farmhouse to be assembled round the large kitchen fire, on a winter's evening. The work of the day was over. The farmer was quietly smoking his pipe and now and then entertaining the children with his oft-repeated tales. The good wife was knitting at his side. At this moment of quiet domestic comfort, the plough boy opened the door, and cried out in great alarm, 'Master, master, there are thieves in the yard.' All is immediate confusion. The farmer rushes to the closet to get his lantern—he supplies it with candle—and runs out, holding the light up to *his head*, and advancing with *cautious* steps in pursuit of the deprodators. In the yard, the wheelbarrow has been improperly left, and over it the farmer tumbles. Why does he fall? Not because he is without light, but because he did not use it properly—so it is with the heathen.

On another occasion, after returning from the country where he had been preaching, he referred to the steamboat on which he had travelled.

How delightful it was to see the fine vessel dashing through the waters, with the wind and tide against her; but how did she accomplish the great work? Oh, it was the fire within her that produced the power; and how does a poor believer swim against the tide of his corruptions, and stem the torrent of worldly opposition? Oh, it is the power of the Spirit within him which is constantly supplied in answer to his fervent and persevering prayers.

Many of his illustrations and sermons made deep impressions on his congregations and were remembered for many years afterwards. Wilberforce once heard him say, 'I would not give a farthing for that man's religion whose cat and dog were not the better for it.' Wilberforce went on to say that, 'while probably everything else he said that evening was long ago forgotten, no one could forget this.' Once, when he was touring Yorkshire, he visited an old friend, who said to him, 'Mr Hill, it is just *sixty-five* years since I first heard you preach, and I remember your text, and part of your sermon.' Rowland was delighted and surprised, saying, 'It is more than I do.'

You told us [his friend continued] that some people were very squeamish about the delivery of different ministers, who preached the same gospel. You said, suppose you were attending to hear a will read, where you expected a legacy to be left you, would you employ the time when it was reading in criticising the manner in which the lawyer read it? No, you would not; you would be giving all ear to hear if anything was left to you, and how much it was. That is the way I would advise you to hear the gospel.

Sometimes the energy of his manner was overwhelming. Once at Wotton he was completely carried away by his feelings and, raising himself up to his full height, exclaimed,

Because I am in earnest, men call me an enthusiast; but I am not; mine are the words of truth and soberness. When I first came into this part of the country, I was walking on yonder hill; I saw a gravel pit fall in, and bury three human beings alive. I lifted up my voice for help so loudly, that I was heard in the town below, at a distance of a mile; help came, and rescued two of the poor sufferers. No one called me an *enthusiast* then; and when I see eternal destruction ready to fall upon poor sinners, and about to entomb them irrecoverably in an overwhelming mass of woe, and call aloud on them to escape, shall I be called an enthusiast now? No, sinner, I am not an enthusiast in so doing; I call on thee *aloud* to fly for refuge, to the hope set before thee in the gospel of Christ Jesus.

Warnings such as the above 'came from a heart awed with the terrors of the Lord' and his invitations to turn to Christ were poured forth with the tears of tenderness of one who yearned over the salvation of souls.

In his youthful zeal he was accustomed to 'stamp violently with his foot, thump his Bible, and even stretch himself over his desk and strike the foot of the pulpit'.

On one occasion a friend, who had travelled with him in Scotland, said to him, 'I shall never forget that sermon you preached [many years ago] in the old church at K—. It was an excellent discourse.'

'Yes,' replied the veteran, with a kind of frown, 'I remember the devil told me that before I left the pulpit.'

'At any rate,' said the friend, 'it was followed by the divine blessing. There was a great awakening among the people.'

'That is the grand thing,' he replied, 'it is a poor sermon however noisy or eloquent, that merely tickles the ear without touching the heart.'

'You thundered away at a fine rate that morning. I will venture to say that the pulpit cushion had not received such a castigation for many years, for it was a very inanimate minister who stately preached there. In a few minutes you raised such a cloud of dust as nearly hid you from my view. Some who could not gain admittance, told me they heard you very well in the churchyard.'

'Ah,' replied Mr Hill, thoughtfully, 'things have altered since then. The bull-dog has got old and cannot bark quite so loud. It is a great mercy that he can bark at all.'

Hardly a Sunday passed without some notice of the success of his preaching. John Ellis moved to London in 1786, at the age of nineteen. Under Rowland's ministry he was brought 'to lie at the foot of the cross', where for weeks he doubted the possibility of salvation. Eventually he received joy and peace in believing. In his own words, he said, 'For weeks my comforts, nay, transports, were such that I felt gazing upon Immanuel as the chief among ten thousand, and altogether lovely.' He became a member of Rowland's church and, with his approbation, started preaching the gospel. He emigrated to America in November 1795 and settled in Pennsylvania.

One man, under deep conviction of sin from listening to Rowland, handed him a slip of paper in the pulpit, on which was written in a beautiful hand:

Will God indeed hear prayer for a hardened and impenitent sinner, who *would* mourn over his vileness, but *cannot*; who *longs* to approach his mercy seat, and to draw near to the table of the Lord, but *dares not*; whose soul is darkness, and his heart cold within him! Oh! that Jesus would shine into his soul, and chase away the clouds of sin that involve it, that he may no longer go sighing all the day long, as they that have no hope, and no consolation.

Rowland invited this man to a private interview. After a long delay, he went with a trembling heart to see his pastor, who led him to Christ.

Rowland was fond of mentioning a woman in Kent, who was also led to the Saviour through his ministry. Before her conversion she had had an uncontrollable temper, which made her household miserable, but when she met Jesus, she started to watch and pray against her sin. 'At times, when she found it rising, she would quietly turn to one corner of the room and there, for a moment, present the secret prayer, and drop the holy penitential tear, and return to her family with a countenance sweet as that of an angel.' Rowland then added, 'Her unbelieving husband would say, "I don't know much about religion myself, but this I know, that it has done my wife a vast deal of good."'

When Matthew Wilks was preaching the funeral sermon of Samuel Foyster, one of the managers of the Tabernacle and Tottenham Court Chapel, he said, 'Rambling about from one place to another, he went into Tottenham Court Chapel and went behind a pillar that he might not be seen. The Rev. Rowland Hill was preaching. The Lord saw him there, and met with him... He showed his fear of God in the management of his family... He made religion pleasant to his family by kindness and affection.' John Newton once told Pratman of Barnard Castle that he knew for certain that Rowland had once preached a sermon for a Baptist minister, who afterwards received twelve people into the church as fruits of that sermon.

Sometimes many years went by before Rowland heard about the results of his ministry. A close friend and fellow traveller in Christ's cause, Thomas Jackson, said on one occasion, after Rowland had preached to a crowded congregation for the Missionary Society in Princes Street Chapel, Devonport,

...the people had withdrawn, and the deacons and a few friends had retired, with Mr H., into the vestry, when two tall, venerable looking men, upwards of seventy years of age, appeared at the vestry door. After a short pause they entered, arm in arm, and advanced towards Mr Hill, when one of them said, with some degree of trepidation, 'Sir, will you permit two old sinners to have the honour to shake you by the hand?'

He replied (with some reserve), 'Yes, sir.'

When one of these gentlemen (the other hanging on his arm) took his hand, kissed it, bathed it with tears, and said, 'Sir, do you remember preaching on the spot where this chapel now stands fifty years ago?'

'Yes I do,' was the reply.

The old man then proceeded to say, 'Oh Sir! never can the dear friend who has hold of my arm, or myself, forget that sermon; we were then two careless young men in his majesty's dock-yard, posting to destruction as fast as time and sin could convey us thither. Having heard that an interesting young clergyman was to preach out of doors, we determined to go and have some fun; accordingly we loaded our pockets with stones, intending to pelt you; but, sir, when you arrived, our courage failed, and as soon as you engaged in prayer we were so deeply impressed that we looked at each other and trembled. When you named your text, and began to speak, the word came with power to our hearts; the big tears rolled down our cheeks; we put our hands into our pockets, and dropped the stones one after another, until they were all gone; for God had taken the stone out of our hearts. When the service was over we retired, but our hearts were too full to speak until we came near to our lodgings, when my friend at my elbow said, "John, this will not do; we are both wrong; good night." This was all he could utter; he retired to his apartment, I to mine; but neither of us dared to go to bed, lest we should awake in hell; and from that time, sir, we humbly hope we were converted to God, who, of his infinite mercy, has kept us in his ways to the present moment; and we thought, sir, if you would permit us, after the lapse of half a hundred years, to have the pleasure of shaking you by the hand before we go home, it would be the greatest honour that could be conferred on us.'

Mr Hill was deeply affected; the tears rolled down his venerable cheeks in quick succession; he fell on the necks of the old men quite in the patriarchal style, and there you might have seen them, locked in each other's arms, weeping tears of holy joy and gratitude to the Father of mercies.

The substance of Rowland's preaching consisted of the three Rs: *Ruin* by the fall, *Redemption* by the cross of Christ, and *Regeneration* by the Holy Spirit. 'These are the doctrines which humble the sinner, exalt the Saviour and promote holiness.' Once, when examining a young man for the ministry, he said, 'Well, the gospel is a good milch cow, she gives plenty of milk. I never write my sermons. I first give a pull at justification, then a plug at adoption, and afterwards a bit at sanctification; and so, in one way or another, I fill my pail with the gospel milk.' Jay said, 'He fell into no errors. He embraced no whims. He made no new discoveries in religion. He never supposed any were to *be* made.'

There was not one of his sermons 'but more than touched upon the sole theme of the Apostle's ministry, "Jesus Christ and him crucified"—"the Lord our righteousness and strength"; whatever his subject was, it was sure, before its close, to exhale forth something of the "savour of the Redeemer's knowledge"'. He preached the depravity of man's nature, which, according to Sidney, during his early life, 'drew down upon him and his friends every species of obloquy, hatred and persecution from those who forgot that they were giving, by their violence, a practical demonstration of the very truths they were contending against'. About 1803, when preaching at Whitefield's Tabernacle, Rowland said, 'Had I kept within bounds, and spoke of sin as if there was little harm in it, I was assured of considerable preferment; but I could not do so, and they turned me out. If you wish many clergymen to be more useful, you must pray that they may be turned out also.'

He fully admitted divine sovereignty, but held that doctrine in balance with the personal responsibility of individuals. He believed in the effectual calling of the saints and their final perseverance, and in the doctrine of election, but he did not hold that the election of some to eternal life necessarily implied the reprobation of others. In his sermon on the death of his friend James Rouquet, he cried,

Every moment brings you nearer to eternity. How then will you bear to stand in the presence of a holy sin-avenging God, whose authority you have defied, and whose gospel you have hitherto despised? O that some alarming word might constrain you to fly, hastily to fly, from the wrath to come! Death and destruction alone are before you, while you continue living in sin. But thanks be to God for his unspeakable gift! Christ is revealed as the salvation of the lost; whosoever cometh shall certainly be received... Such is the adorable Christ that is now ready to snatch you as brands from the burning, and make you standing monuments of mercy and salvation... O that I could prevail! I point you to that lovely sacrifice, the Lamb of God that taketh away the sins of the world; to his mercy I commend you, and may his salvation be the happy portion of all your hearts.

James Rouquet

He was a strong supporter of the law as a rule of life. 'I follow the law,' he said, *'from* the life within me, not *for* life.' When Sidney entered the ministry, Rowland strongly urged him to begin with declaring the law as a first step of leading sinners to Christ. He summarized his views on the extent of the atonement, by saying to a friend, 'I love to look at the atonement as a glorious plan, which enables the Father, consistently with all his glorious attributes, "to be just, and yet the justifier of him that believeth in Jesus".'

He was very practical in his preaching and always tried to make what he said come alive. Once he recommended to his friends who had troublesome tempers to put 1 Corinthians chapter 13 between their bread and butter at breakfast time and they would find the advantage of it all day. When the Religious Tract Society published *The Important Discovery; or, Temper is Everything*, he mentioned from the pulpit that he had bought many copies of this tract and that as some of his hearers were troubled in their tempers, he would be happy to give them a copy, if they would call on him at the chapel house. Not surprisingly, no one asked for a copy of the little book!

He once gave a memorable illustration of the necessity for a Christian to make the gospel his all in all.

I saw the other day a little boy with a small fish in his hand, which he was trying to keep alive by putting every now and then a drop of water into its mouth. All was in vain; the finny creature soon died. Had he sent it forth into the full stream, it would have recovered its strength and gone swimming joyously away. Thus it is with the

Christian. An occasional drop of the gospel cannot keep his soul alive. No, brethren, plunge into the depths of the waters of life, and your souls shall live.

In his preaching he stressed the importance of prayer in the life of every believer and used many natural pictures to illustrate his point.

We know that the infinite God cannot be moved or actually drawn nearer to us by prayer, but prayer draws the Christian nearer to God...

The Christian is therefore enjoined to *pray without ceasing*; not that he can be always engaged in the positive act, but he ought to have what I call *a holy aptitude for prayer*. The bird is not always on the wing, but he is ready to fly in an instant; so the believer is not always on the wing of prayer, but he has such a gracious aptitude for this exercise, that he is prepared in an instant, when in danger or need, to fly for refuge to his God.

In all the avocations of time, the child of God will never lose sight of his heavenly Father. I have often seen a little child following his parent in the fields, and stooping now and then to gather a few flowers. He looks up and sees him at a distance; the little creature runs and gets up to him again, afraid he should go too far away. So the Christian, while gathering a few flowers from the world, suffers his God to be often a distance from him; but the instant he perceives that he is left alone, he runs to reach again his Father, Protector and Friend.

At times the rapid succession of ideas that flowed into his mind made what he said appear ludicrous and almost wild, although most of the stories told about his pulpit peculiarities are without foundation. He rarely resorted to humour to attract the attention of his congregation, except for the sake of some particular purpose. To those who found it hard to give to the Lord's work, he said somewhat cheekily, 'There is a perpetual frost in the pockets of some wealthy people; as soon as they put their hands into them they are frozen, and unable to draw out their purses. Had I my way, I would hang all misers, but the reverse of the common mode; I would hang them up by their heels, that their money might run out of their pockets, and make a famous scramble for you to pick up and put in the plate.'

Chapter 22

Charles Spurgeon in *Eccentric Preachers* mentioned the time Rowland went to Collyer's chapel at Peckham:

He spoke for twenty-five minutes in a strain of deepest solemnity, but at last the real man broke out, and for the next quarter of an hour quaintness came to the front. In the vestry, at the close, he observed that he had over and over again resolved to utter no expression which could excite a smile, but, said he, 'I find it's no use. Though my very life depended upon it, I could not help myself.' He never went out of his way for odd and striking sayings, he even strove to avoid them, but they were natural to him, and he was not himself without them. Do we blame the man for being himself? We blame him not, but commend him. Originality is not to be censured, but encouraged.

On one occasion at Surrey Chapel Rowland copied one of George Whitefield's antics. Rowland took for his text Philippians 4:13. He said, 'I can do all things...' then paused, before adding, 'That I deny! I'll bet you half a crown, Paul, that it is not true.' He pulled the coin out of his pocket and placed it on the Bible in front of him. He then said, 'But stay, let us look a little further into the text.' He read on: '... through Christ which strengthened me.' He shook his head and remarked, 'Ah, that alters the question—it's a drawn bet,' and putting the money back in his pocket, he carried on with the sermon.

One member of his congregation said that in the pulpit Rowland 'seemed conscious of standing on holy ground, and his words were solemn, weighty, and impressive', although 'he sometimes used expressions that created a smile'. As for those 'vulgar and absurd utterances, which many were fond of putting into his mouth, they rest upon no foundation of truth whatever'. Rowland's chief complaint was that 'people would not allow him to be a gentleman'. In the twelve years that this man had been a member of Surrey Chapel, he had 'never heard him utter a sentence unbecoming an ambassador of Christ, or the sanctity of the pulpit'. Still, he thought these 'foolish reports' might have done more good than real mischief, because many were induced by them to come from distant villages and towns to hear the eccentric preacher, and 'not a few were savingly impressed with the power of the truth'. He then related the following story:

One Sabbath morning, as I was about to proceed to my accustomed place of worship, a female friend waited upon me, in company with two farming men from a distance. She told me they had a great desire to hear Mr Hill, and requested that I would take them with me and get them seated in a favourable position. I willingly undertook this commission, and, as we proceeded on our way, the two men asked me many questions about 'Sir Rowland', as they called him, and informed me of many things they had heard respecting him.

'They do tell me,' observed one, 'that he should say, religion were loike a round of beef; it be coot and coome agin.'

'Well,' I replied, 'he often makes use of very homely expressions, but I do not remember ever having heard him make that remark.' Strangely enough, that very morning we were favoured with something near of kin to it. I took the men into my pew and for some time they seemed to take the greatest interest in everything that was going on; but when the venerable preacher ascended the pulpit, every other object ceased to attract their attention.

'There he be,' said one to the other, 'there he be.'

'Ees,' replied his companion, 'how happy he do look.'

His subject was, 'the Gospel of our salvation,' and as he proceeded with his discourse my two friends began to be evidently excited. The fullness and freeness of that salvation—was set forth in burning words, and their excitement increased. 'It is free,' he exclaimed, 'free as the air you breathe. And it is as full as it is free. There is enough for all. I never heard a man say to his neighbour, "Don't you breathe so much air; if you do, there will not be enough for me to breathe." No, there is sufficient for everyone, and all are invited to come to the gospel feast. "In my Father's house is bread enough and to spare." It is cut and come again.'

At this the delighted countrymen rose to their feet and stretched themselves forward as if unable any longer to control their feelings. I became alarmed lest their emotions should find vent in some audible exclamation, so I gently touched the one next to me and smilingly motioned him to resume his seat. To my great relief he immediately complied, and the other following his example, after he had given a few violent nods of satisfaction, I was enabled once more to breathe freely.

After the service they warmly thanked me for the little kindness rendered them, and spoke of the pleasure they should afford their neighbours when they returned home and reported how they had seen and heard 'Sir Rowland Hill'.

Spurgeon, who in many ways was similar to Rowland, said this in his defence:

Mr Hill may have allowed his humour too much liberty, perhaps he did, but this was better than smothering it and all other faculties, as many do, beneath a huge feather-bed of stupid formalism...

Mr Hill's name is very sweet in South London, and if you chance to meet with one of his old hearers, it will do your heart good to see how his eyes will sparkle at the mention of his name. He made religion a delight and the worship of God a pleasure; yea, he made the very memory of it to be a joy for ever to the hearts of the aged as they recall the days of their youth when Rowland Hill—dear old Rowland Hill as they like to call him—was in his glory.

This extract serves as a fitting conclusion to this study of Rowland's life and work.